If there is anyone who can move people to action, it is my friend Sammy Rodriguez. By the time you finish reading the last page of this book, I trust you will see yourself as a victor, not a victim of your circumstances. No longer will you allow others to define you. Like the paralyzed man described in John 5, you will boldly pick up your mat and walk—ready to embrace the abundant life God has planned for you!

—JAMES ROBISON
PRESIDENT AND FOUNDER, LIFE OUTREACH INTERNATIONAL

Sammy is a good friend and one of my favorite people. His new book, *You Are Next*, is filled with personal stories woven together with Scripture and insights drawn directly from his unique career, adventures, and experiences. If you're feeling stuck, unfulfilled, overlooked, or like you're constantly falling short, the principles found in this book will help you find healing and freedom and give you the power to change not only your life but also your legacy!

—ROBERT MORRIS
LEAD SENIOR PASTOR, GATEWAY CHURCH
BEST-SELLING AUTHOR OF *THE BLESSED LIFE*,
FREQUENCY, AND *BEYOND BLESSED*

This is less a Christian self-help book than it is a prophetic proclamation over your future! Using examples both from Scripture and from his own remarkable life experience, Samuel paints a powerful word picture about how to once and for all break the cycle of your present and be released from your past so God can "empower you to do what you could not do before." If you feel like you've been in a years-long holding pattern, believing God for certain change but not seeing it materialize, this book was written for you.

—MATTHEW CROUCH
PRESIDENT, TRINITY BROADCASTING NETWORK

It's time to have faith enough to hear the voice of Jesus saying to you, "Be healed. Pick up your mat and walk!" If you find yourself stuck in failures, your family heritage, doubts, or insecurities, the mat pick up right now is this book as Pastor Sam inspires and guides you to have faith enough to believe God's promises for your life. When I need a spiritual shot in the arm, I call Pastor Sam to hear same thoughts and words contained in this book and to remember God's unfailing, unrelenting, and unending love for us all.

—PAULA WHITE-CAIN
SENIOR PASTOR, NEW DESTINY CHRISTIAN CENTER

You Are Next needs to be the next book you pick up. Pastor Samuel Rodriguez walks the talk, living a life above the norm. Nobody tells it like Pastor Samuel. His enthusiasm, his faith, his wisdom, his humor, and his God-given personality and character overflow on these pages. In his new book you will be inspired through his stories and illustrations and encouraged to look up and step up into the extraordinary life God has for you. You are next.

—PETER MORTLOCK
FOUNDER AND SENIOR PASTOR, CITY IMPACT CHURCH

Sammy Rodriguez is a gifted communicator—he paints pictures with words. In *You Are Next* Sammy combines excellent exegesis with personal illustrations that will motivate you to live a life above a level of mediocrity. Do yourself and those you lead a favor by reading this book. Who knows? You might experience your own miracle as you read this inspiring work.

—PASTOR DOUG CLAY
GENERAL SUPERINTENDENT,
GENERAL COUNCIL OF THE ASSEMBLIES OF GOD

For anyone who might feel stuck, unfulfilled, overlooked, let down, constantly falling short, or simply just not able to get to the next level—this book is for you! Real, relevant, revelatory, and refreshing, *You Are Next* is a must read.

—JEDIDIAH THURNER
CHIEF STRATEGY OFFICER, MISSIONS.ME

I am so grateful for Rev. Samuel Rodriguez! God has raised him up as a powerful prophetic voice to our nation for this generation. beautifully written book, *You Are Next*, Rev. Samuel tal the story of the healing of the paralyzed man at the pool of Bethesda. In each chapter of this book we are invited, encouraged, and challenged to respond to God's promise of a new and better season in our lives. We learn that we can be free from the crippling traumas of the past and the disabling beliefs and attitudes of our present. Rev. Samuel is an incredibly gifted communicator—both in speech and in writing. This book takes us on a journey from freedom from the past to having a destiny for our future. By sharing great insight into the biblical story, Rev. Samuel builds faith in the reader that God can and will do the same things for them. Every page of this extraordinary book is filled with revelation and hope that will inspire and equip you. It's time to take up your mat and boldly walk into the future God has prepared for you!

—Dr. Michael Maiden
Senior Pastor, Church for the Nations

There is no more important Christian voice in the world than that of Rev. Samuel Rodriguez.

—Rev. Johnnie Moore
Author, Activist,
Founder and CEO, The KAIROS Company

You Are Next is a stirring prophetic invitation for every person to embrace their divine destiny with unshakable conviction and confidence. Rev. Samuel's ability to relate so broadly and articulate so brilliantly means that everyone can potentially relate to every point! By weaving his inspirational journey with bold declarations of truth, this book will pull you in before pulling you out! It won't just fascinate you with facts; it will fuel you with faith!

—Mark Varughese
Senior Leader, Kingdomcity

Unapologetically confronting the most paramount need in our generation, my friend Samuel Rodriguez has brilliantly encapsulated the spirit of empowerment by refuting and nullifying any prevalent or dormant argument for complacency. We all need this book. At least one chapter has your story, your name, and your victory within its pages. No more excuses. You are next!

—SERGIO DE LA MORA
LEAD PASTOR, CORNERSTONE CHURCH OF SAN DIEGO,
AUTHOR, *PARADOX*

Sammy Rodriguez is a world-impacting leader and outstanding communicator. His unique insight will not only empower you but also propel you to new levels of greatness and influence in everything you do. I thoroughly recommend this book!

—RUSSELL EVANS
SENIOR PASTOR, PLANETSHAKERS

The book *You are Next* is a much-needed read, particularly for believers who feel stuck, hopeless, and unable to advance in different aspects of their lives. Samuel Rodriguez does an exceptional job presenting real-life scenarios and aligning them with the truth of God's Word in order to change mindsets. The book also challenges readers to recognize who they are in Christ, to apply His promises in their everyday life, and to never give up because those who persevere are indeed next!

—JOHN K. JENKINS SR.
PASTOR, FIRST BAPTIST CHURCH, GLENARDEN, MD

YOU ARE NEXT

SAMUEL RODRIGUEZ

CHARISMA
HOUSE

Visit the author's website at PastorSam.com and youarenextbook.com.

Library of Congress Cataloging-in-Publication Data:
An application to register this book for cataloging has been submitted to the Library of Congress.
International Standard Book Number: 978-1-62999-591-5
E-book ISBN: 978-1-62999-592-2

This publication is translated in Spanish under the title *Usted es el próximo*, copyright © 2019 by Samuel Rodriguez, published by Casa Creación, a Charisma Media company. All rights reserved.

While the author has made every effort to provide accurate internet addresses at the time of publication, neither the publisher nor the author assumes any responsibility for errors or for changes that occur after publication. Further, the publisher does not have any control over and does not assume any responsibility for author or third-party websites or their content.

19 20 21 22 23 — 987654321
Printed in the United States of America

I DEDICATE THIS BOOK TO
MY PARENTS, SAMUEL AND
ELIZABETH, FOR ALWAYS
BELIEVING THAT I WAS
NEXT! LOVE YOU!

CONTENTS

FOREWORD

WHAT AN HONOR it is to pen these few words commending and recommending this book of hope and promise written by my dear friend Sammy Rodriguez. Sammy is a voice for this generation, and I have never heard him speak when I didn't come away excited and filled with hope and expectation. This book is no different. It is real, raw, and honest, and the powerful truths Sammy unpacks will bring an entirely new perspective to the challenges life brings using real-life examples and the struggles we all face.

There is a reason he is the president of the National Hispanic Christian Leadership Conference (NHCLC), the organization recognized and identified by the *New York Times*, the *Wall Street Journal*, *Christianity Today*, NBC, Telemundo, Univision, Fox News, CNN, and a number of additional media outlets as America's largest and most influential Hispanic/Latino Christian organization with over forty thousand certified member churches in the United States and Latin America. There is a reason he is asked to come and lend counsel and prayer to some of the most influential men and women in the world. There is a reason presidents seek his wisdom and pastors praise his impact and relevance in every kind of congregation and across denominational lines.

Beyond his ability to lead and provide timely counsel, I know of no other author or pastor that has the ability to paint a picture with words the way Sammy Rodriguez can. In *You Are Next* Sammy Rodriguez unpacks an amazing biblical story in a way that all Christians desperately need to hear. He shares powerful insights the Lord has given him for destroying the enemy's plan to keep you sidelined. You'll be encouraged to break free from the cycles that have kept you bound and to see your circumstances in a whole new way. Sammy is an encourager and an exhorter. He not only has the ability to lift your eyes up when you are down, but he also has that rare ability to lead you from the valley of despair and speak purpose and hope and passion into you for the victories that are to come.

I'm very excited Sammy has written this book, especially for the hour we are in. I believe the timing of its release is not an accident. I believe we've just entered a season in which God is pouring out more blessing, more favor, and more of Himself in our lives. Wouldn't you like to have more of God's presence in your life and in the lives of your children and grandchildren? God is pouring out more of Himself, and it's your turn to receive. That is what I'm believing for your life, for your spouse, and for your children, and that is why I wholeheartedly recommend that you set aside the time to walk through the pages ahead.

In *You Are Next* God is setting before you a challenge to receive a better life, a holy life, a God-ordained life. You can stay in your complacent, "if-only" mentality, making excuses for your condition and depending on others to bring you to the edge of your miracle. Or you can stand up, put the devil in his place, live victoriously, dream courageously, live passionately, engage tenaciously, and live the powerful life you've been seeking! Are you ready? If so, then you are next!

—Jentezen Franklin
Senior Pastor, Free Chapel
New York Times Best-Selling Author

ACKNOWLEDGMENTS

I AM GRATEFUL FOR my team and support staff; the love of my life (my wife of twenty-nine years, Eva); Dudley Deffs (therapist and scribe); Steve (Esteban) Strang for twenty years of faithful friendship; Ned Clements; and Debbie Marrie for making it happen.

You are next!

—SAMUEL RODRIGUEZ
LEAD PASTOR, NEW SEASON
NHCLC PRESIDENT
AUTHOR OF *SHAKE FREE*
EXECUTIVE PRODUCER OF *BREAKTHROUGH*

PREFACE

IMAGINE SITTING IN the same spot on the ground day after day. You cannot get on your feet without assistance from other people. You have paralysis in both legs and need help with many of the basic functions that most people take for granted, such as bathing, dressing, and preparing meals. You feel powerless most of the time, at the mercy of a crippling physical condition that has plagued you for almost forty years.

At times you feel angry and resentful, even bitter, as you watch others casually stroll by without even a glance your way. Other times you feel so desperate as you cling to the last gossamer strand of hope for your life to change. You have heard of a place where miracles happen, where apparently a heavenly angel skims the surface of one of the temple pools. Right after the angel departs, the waters ripple with motion and drench the next person who manages to wade into the pool with miraculous healing.

You have been coming to this miraculous spot for years and years. But you move far too slowly to ever be the first one in the water after it has been stirred by an angel. You have watched others shriek with joy as injured limbs become whole, as diseased bodies return to health, as eyes and ears once blind and deaf now see and hear. It has become almost too painful to watch others receive what you long to have, what you struggle to continue to hope for, while each day, the muscles in your legs atrophy and weaken just a little more. Each day, your hope withers.

Then one day a stranger comes by and asks you the oddest question, "Do you want to get well?" It almost insults you at first, but then you think perhaps He does not realize your condition or the extent of the problem logistically. You try to explain that every so often an angel stirs up the waters, and the first person to go into the water experiences his or her corresponding healing or miracle. Even as you speak, you wonder if perhaps this stranger—He certainly looks young and strong—perhaps can finally help carry you to be the first one into the pool.

But He does not even offer.

Instead He does something no one has ever dared.

He tells you to get up and walk...

Chapter One

YOU ARE NEXT...

TO BREAK THE CYCLE OF DEPENDENCY

Today's complacency is
tomorrow's captivity.

WHEN OUR KIDS were small, my wife and I could not wait to take them to Disneyland—not because we wanted them to get caught up in the hype of visiting a theme park with cartoon and movie characters as much as we wanted them to experience the joy of visiting "the happiest place on earth." Growing up in Pennsylvania, I had always wanted to go to Disney World, but our family could not afford it. As a father myself living in California, I loved being able to take my family to Disneyland and enjoy an experience I did not have as a kid.

Among the many memorable moments that day, one stands out after all these years. If you have ever visited a theme park, then you know much of your day consists of "hurry up and wait." Everyone gets so excited about being there and enjoying all the rides and attractions. But after you enter the park and race to the first stop on your list, you usually have to wait in line, and wait some more, sometimes waiting an hour or longer for your turn to experience a ride lasting all of three minutes.

We had the same experience, and I have to say, with young children it seemed even longer. By early afternoon the beautiful Southern California day had become hot and sticky. The kids were getting tired and cranky. But all of us wanted to do the Indiana Jones ride, so there we stood, along with several hundred other equally enthusiastic park goers. As the lines crawled along, we could not wait to turn the corner up ahead and, we assumed, experience the thrills waiting behind the cavernous mine shaft where the ride began.

But when we finally reached what appeared to be the front of the line, we turned the corner only to see another labyrinth of chains filled with more people than we ever imagined. We were not even halfway there! Our daughter groaned, "We will never get to the front!" I tried to reassure her while struggling to imagine how this ride could possibly be worth the wait unless Harrison Ford himself sat next to us in the Temple of Doom.

"Daddy, look!" my son said. "I see a way in with no line!"

My gaze followed his pointed finger to a nearby doorway. "Buddy, the park reserves that entrance for people who are hurt or have physical conditions that make it hard for them to wait. People with disabilities or those with special needs use that entrance to get on the ride."

"Well, let's go through that door then because I have a special need. I can't wait any longer!" he said.

My wife and I laughed, but his reaction indicated his seriousness. As sweat trickled down my back, I have to admit the idea tempted me. For a moment I wondered what would happen if I edged my family over to that line where we could just walk in and get on the ride. But I did not.

"I am not sure you have the kind of special need we are talking about," I told him. "That entrance helps people who really need help."

"Like him?" My son pointed at a young man in a wheelchair in the row behind us. I gently lowered my son's hand and smiled in the direction of the young man in question. The man smiled and waved at my son. Wearing sunglasses, a T-shirt, and board shorts, the young man looked like any other twentysomething at the park that day except that his right leg ended at the knee, necessitating the use of the wheelchair.

"Well, yes," I said. "He probably could use that entrance."

Our line began to move a few feet closer.

"Then why doesn't he?" my son said, not about to let the topic drop.

"Excuse me, but I couldn't help but overhear you."

Mortified, I turned to see the young man in the wheelchair now almost directly behind us in the next row. "Sorry," I said. "It's just that—"

"No problem," the man said and smiled. "I understand. It is fine, really. I just overheard your son and wanted to answer his question if I may. My name's Jeff, by the way."

We shook hands, and I introduced myself and the members of my family.

"I do not use the handicapped entrance," Jeff said, "because I do not think of myself as handicapped. Sure, I don't have all of my right leg, but that does not keep me from living my life. I still go to work, play basketball with my friends, and go wherever I want."

"Like Disneyland!" my son said.

"Exactly!" Jeff said. "You are only limited by the way you see your circumstances—not by the circumstances themselves."

TENDENCY FOR DEPENDENCY

Our encounter with Jeff made quite the impression that day—not just on my son but on me as well. On the one hand, there we were, my son and I, being tempted to take a shortcut not intended for us simply because we were impatient. We knew we did not have a disability or a special need for a shorter line and a special entrance, but nonetheless, we did not want to wait for our turn.

Our new friend Jeff, on the other hand, provided an amazing contrast. Presumably a military veteran, he had lost half his leg and consequently had to adjust to life with this new limitation. While many people might be tempted to feel sorry for themselves, to feel entitled to take shortcuts and receive special attention, this young man had taken the opposite direction. He had shifted his attitude to one that refused to see himself as a victim of circumstances or as someone less than who God had made him. I will never forget his message: "You are only limited by the way you see your circumstances—not by the circumstances themselves."

Please understand that I am not calling people who need special assistance due to limiting conditions victims or in any way a weaker person than someone such as Jeff. I am just pointing out the contrast between two different temptations that day, two sides of the same settle-for-less coin. My son felt it unfair to have to wait in the sweltering heat in such a long line; therefore, he should be able to take the wheelchair accessible entrance. Jeff, someone who obviously could justify taking such a shortcut due to his physical disability, chose not to use the accessible line because of the way it made him feel to do so. He had experienced a brutal, unfair injury yet refused to let it define him or change the strength of his character.

> **"You are only limited by the way you see your circumstances—not by the circumstances themselves."**

We find it easy to grow dependent on what we cannot control in our lives. We find it tempting to view life as unfair and to feel like a victim of our circumstances. And we find it convenient to stay put instead of stepping out in faith. But if we want to break our cycle of dependency and eliminate our excuses, then we have to be willing to accept all that God has for us.

Our tendency for dependency is nothing new. Throughout His public ministry Christ encountered people who often felt trapped by their circumstances or limited by their wounds. He frequently healed people suffering from physical, mental, and spiritual maladies. And with His love, power, and grace Jesus exploded their excuses and ignited their initiative to live by faith, not by sight. His encounter with a man who could not walk—and who apparently did not recognize Jesus—was brief and dramatic but carries enormous implications and application for our lives today. Take a look.

> Later on, there was another festival of the Jews, and Jesus went up to Jerusalem. Near the Sheep Gate in Jerusalem is a pool called Bethesda in Hebrew. It has five colonnades, and under these a large number of sick people were lying—blind, lame, or paralyzed—waiting for the movement of the water. At certain times an angel of the Lord would go down into the pool and stir up the water, and whoever stepped in first after the stirring of the water was healed of whatever disease he had.
>
> One particular man was there who had been ill for 38 years. When Jesus saw him lying there and knew that he had already been there a long time, he asked him, "Do you want to get well?"

The sick man answered him, "Sir, I don't have anyone to put me into the pool when the water is stirred up. While I'm trying to get there, someone else steps down ahead of me."

Jesus told him, "Stand up, pick up your mat, and walk!" The man immediately became well, and he picked up his mat and started walking.

—JOHN 5:1–9, ISV

THE EDGE OF A MIRACLE

First, note the setting described in this scene. Located near the entrance to the temple in Jerusalem known as the Sheep Gate, the pool at Bethesda likely served as a public bath where visitors could cleanse and refresh themselves before going to make their offering before God and worship Him. Archaeologists have confirmed five covered colonnades surrounded the pool, similar to small porches or open-air gazebos along the sides. Knowing that many had been healed of their infirmities when entering the pool right after its waters had been stirred by an angel, a small crowd frequented the site.

As you imagine this scene in your mind, can you see the crowd of people with disabilities? So much suffering and pain; so many broken limbs and disfigured bodies; so many groans of discomfort and cries for help. Sheep and goats bleat in the distance where they can be purchased for sacrifice while the smell of human bodies, decay, and disease mingle with the scent of eucalyptus, mint, and lavender on the warm breeze. Everyone waits, hoping to be the first into the pool once they glimpse its surface shuddering with motion from the invisible angel gracing the pool with its presence.

Then your mind's eye tightens focus like a camera zeroing in on one lone individual. Among the many gathered there—those who could not see, those who could not walk, those who could not move at all—this man was a regular. Scripture says he had not been able to walk for thirty-eight years—more than the span of a generation. While we do not know if he had been coming to the pool for that long, we can safely guess he had.

It must have been like torture for him—lying there, so close to an opportunity for healing but ironically prevented from grasping it by the very infirmity ailing him. The physical ailment for which he desired healing kept him from the wellness right in front of him. So close, at the edge of a miracle, and yet so far away; he had little hope.

Then into the middle of this scene came Jesus, who traveled to Jerusalem and arrived at the temple to celebrate one of the Jewish feast days. Noticing the paralyzed man, Jesus knew he had been in this condition for a long time. And then we get to one of my very favorite details in this scene, the first line of dialogue in the form of Jesus' question: "Do you want to get well?"

Of all the things our Lord could have said, the paralyzed man probably did not expect this! Think about it—why else would this man be stretched out on the ground among so many other wounded, hurting, suffering people? Didn't everyone gather there because they wanted to get well? Only someone either very unobservant or unintelligent might be tempted to ask such an obvious question.

Why in the world would the all-knowing and all-powerful Jesus ask this poor man such a question? It would seem cruel or totally out of touch if you or I were to ask someone on crutches the same question in a doctor's office! What was Jesus up to here? What was His motive in taking this approach with this man and his affliction? Could it be Jesus viewed the paralyzed man's attitude as more pivotal to his healing than whether or not he could reach the pool?

This man had been unable to walk for almost four decades. But based on the Master's question to him, we must wonder if the *obvious* problem was not necessarily the *real* problem hindering this man's recovery and healing. He responded to Jesus not by describing his condition or the cause of it but instead indicated reasons for his inability to experience healing. "Sir," the man said, "I have no one to help me get into the water before someone else beats me to it. I am too slow, and I cannot rush ahead of all the others in need gathered here." I am paraphrasing and elaborating on this man's response found in verse 7, but I do not think I am stretching the point.

The man's reply proves just as fascinating as Jesus' question! Paralyzed and alone, this man thought that above all he needed to find someone to help him get to the pool before the angelically stirred waters settled and lost their healing power. Curiously enough, he did not ask Jesus for help to get into the pool. Instead, he merely described his situation, emphasizing his inability to be healed. The way he saw it, he could never achieve healing on his own even though he had made it to the edge of the pool. Because he had no one to help him, he was paralyzed in a painful emotional purgatory. He could see the means of his restoration but could never reach it.

It seems almost as if this man had resigned himself to a life where what he desired most could be seen but not attained. He had given up on the miracle he saw others experiencing. Even if someone were to help him, he had convinced himself that he would never have enough speed and mobility to reach the pool in time. He would never dare to consider the possibility that a stranger would show up one day and tell him to get up and walk.

He was just stuck with no hope of being unstuck.

He believed the labels others have placed on him, and he could not imagine who he would be if he were no longer disabled.

JUST OUT OF REACH

This paralyzed man's predicament reminds me of a story I heard from a friend. He shared how he had been on vacation in Florida to visit his elderly father. At his father's request they had gone to the greyhound races, where people would bet on which dogs would win against the other canine competitors (a sport that Florida voters recently decided to phase out by the end of 2020). These big, sleek animals have bodies like missiles and are natural hunters who can reach amazing speeds of twenty, thirty, or even forty miles an hour.

My friend does not gamble, and he did not really like seeing animals put in that kind of competitive, high-stakes situation. Nonetheless, though, he admired their graceful beauty as they streaked around the dirt track, chasing a mechanical rabbit that always remained ahead of them. But that day, however, something strange happened. The dogs were lined up and positioned to race, contained in gated lanes until the bell sounded as the mechanical rabbit darted past them.

Only this time something went wrong. The rabbit zoomed by, and the dogs dashed from their lanes, but then about hundred yards later the mechanized bunny malfunctioned and came to a screeching halt. All the spectators gasped and most, including my friend, probably expected the dogs to pounce on the fake rabbit and tear it to bits. But that did not happen. Instead the poor pups became utterly confused and did not know what to do with themselves!

My friend described it as the strangest sight. All eight dogs in the race stopped. A couple sniffed at the broken bunny and then began exploring the fence. Some found a shady spot beneath a billboard at the edge of the track. Another started to whine, clearly confused about what had happened. One even took care of some personal business right in the middle of the track, much to everyone's amusement. But one thing became clear: without a rabbit to chase, the greyhounds lost their motivation for racing. After countless training courses and practice runs chasing after an elusive target, when the dogs faced the object of their pursuit, they did not know what to do with it!

I suspect we often act the same way. We make our lives conditional on something just out of reach. If only we could finish our degree, then we could move forward and get a great job doing what we love. If only we could be noticed for our hard work, then we would get that promotion. If only our spouse could change his or her bad habits, then our marriage would work. If only our kids could beat their addictions, then we could finally quit worrying and enjoy life again. If only we could find the right church, then we would grow in our faith.

If only... if only... if only...

But then what happens when we get our "if only"? We feel lost! We find something else to make the pivot point for our contentment, forward progress, or spiritual growth. Like the greyhounds, we chase after our rabbit but then stumble when we catch it. Like the man at the pool of Bethesda, we wait on someone else to help us get what we want. We become dependent on other people, uncontrollable events, and different circumstances because we feel powerless. We watch others get what we want to have, go where we want to go, experience what we long to do. But we feel alone, and we do not have what we need to attain what we long to have.

We remain paralyzed and watch as others experience the joy that comes from attaining what we so desperately wish we had.

We choose to remain paralyzed.

RUNNING TO WIN

Can you relate to the kind of situation where you depend on someone else or something else for your life to change? How many times have you accomplished a goal or fulfilled a dream only to experience incredible disappointment?

I am a lifelong runner and have always loved to compete in 5K and 10K races. The exercise keeps me in shape and allows me to enjoy some private time with God to pray, listen, and reflect.

A few years back, at the encouragement of some of my running buddies, I agreed to sign up for a marathon about six months away. For most runners, including me, completing a marathon— or many of them—is a lifelong goal, a measurable way to know you have improved enough to compete at the highest level.

I trained and gradually began running longer and longer distances in preparation for the 26.2-mile course looming before me. I had always been more of a speed guy, so I did not enjoy going from a faster-paced short run to a slower-paced test of my endurance. But the challenge energized me, and soon I felt more and more confident that I could finish the marathon.

As I pushed myself through miles seventeen, eighteen, and nineteen, which for me seemed to be the most grueling, I often imagined myself triumphantly crossing the finish line. My wife and kids would be there cheering me on, congratulating me, and celebrating my accomplishment. I could envision the scene clearly, and it motivated me to complete many a workout in anticipation of race day.

But on race day when I crossed the finish line, my joy did not last very long. Yes, Eva and my kids were there, excited to see me in my moment of glory and proud of the work I did to cross that line. But after rehydrating with lots of Gatorade and enjoying a huge plate of pasta, I felt disappointed. Now what did I have to look forward to? Like those greyhound dogs with no rabbit to chase, I needed a new goal. But even as I plotted my next race—a triathlon, maybe?—I knew the result would always be the same.

Growing up, I often heard my mother say, "Be careful what you ask for—you might get it!" I did not understand what she meant at the time, but later her meaning sank in. If you do not pursue God, you will always be disappointed. Although I pursued Him completely, I still experienced the letdown that comes from attaining something I had allowed to define me.

I had to come to terms with what I expected—and why. Otherwise, it did not matter how many races I ran. I could win the Boston Marathon, but it would not be enough.

Whether we find ourselves paralyzed and lying on the ground or running a marathon, we can only break our dependency on defining ourselves by our circumstances if we wrestle with Jesus' question.

I ask you, my friend, Do you want to get well?

VICTORS NOT VICTIMS

Paul summed up my marathon experience quite well by using the way we race as a metaphor for our relationship with God and our pursuit of Him: "Do you not know that in a race all the runners run, but only one gets the prize? Run in such a way as to get the prize. Everyone who competes in the games goes into strict training. They do it to get a crown that will not last, but we do it to get a crown that will last forever" (1 Cor. 9:24–25). He knew firsthand that no matter how significant our achievement or how devastating our loss, we win our race of faith by focusing on Christ.

I fear that too often we remain dependent on "if only" and "what if" in our lives. We come up with reasons why we cannot experience the full, abundant life Jesus told us He came to bring (John 10:10). We wait on someone else to help us while feeling sorry for ourselves because we cannot make it to the source of healing on our own. On one extreme we make excuses for taking ourselves out of life's races, while on the other we chase after our gold medals and then wonder why they do not satisfy us.

We find the solution, of course, in breaking the cycle of dependency in our lives and taking responsibility for doing what God tells us to do. And I am not sure Jesus could be any clearer in His command to the paralyzed man—and to us today! "Get up! Pick up your mat and walk," our Savior said (John 5:8).

While this paralyzed man with tunnel vision focused solely on his physical disability and inability to receive healing, Jesus, of course, saw a much bigger need. Our Lord knew that this poor man could not be truly healed until he let go of the preoccupation that had defined him for the previous thirty-eight years. Jesus understood how this painful condition had become the center of the man's identity. The fact that we do not know his name—that he is identified at first only as an invalid—tells us as much.

What deficit have you allowed to define you? What limp, injury, or disease do you carry in your soul even though your body recovered from your wounds? How do you answer Jesus' question to you: "Do you want to get well?"

Before you answer with an automatic affirmative, I challenge you to stop and think about what you know to be true based on how you have lived your life until now. Christ offers you the same healing He gifted to the man that day at the pool of Bethesda. But will you do anything necessary to receive it? Will you choose to pick up your mat and walk? Or will you continue waiting on someone else to carry you to your miracle?

If we genuinely desire wellness—and I am talking about health and wholeness in all areas of our lives: physical, mental, emotional, spiritual—we must be willing to let go of the labels we have allowed to define us. We must move beyond the barriers we allow to limit us from day to day. We must choose to stop seeing ourselves as victims of our circumstances and instead start seeing our circumstances as subject to the authority and healing power of Jesus Christ. We are victors, not victims!

We also have to let go of the qualifications we might be tempted to tack on to Jesus' command to get up and walk. From my own experience and what I have observed in the lives of others, we often make excuses even after we have accepted Christ and have the Holy Spirit within us. We have the gift, but we do not want to open it! We have the power, but we do not want to welcome it! We have our miracle, but we do not know how to move forward after being paralyzed by dependency for so long.

> **We must choose to stop seeing ourselves as victims of our circumstances and instead start seeing our circumstances as subject to the authority and healing power of Jesus Christ.**

We want healing, but we want it on our terms. "Yes, Lord, I want to be well as long as I do not experience too much pain or pay too much. I want to be well, but I really do not want to face the uncertainty of change." But healing and miracles might not necessarily be offered on our terms. If they were, many of us would always be waiting on someone to carry us to our miracle instead of accepting the miracle Jesus offers us where we are.

I love that the paralyzed man did exactly what the Lord asked him to do and immediately and instantaneously experienced complete healing. Atrophied muscles tingled with strength and twisted tendons straightened. The man stood and realized he did not need anyone to carry him anywhere! Jesus offered healing with no strings, no contingencies, no rituals. This man could have responded to Jesus' command to stand up with sarcasm, bitterness, anger, or fear. But that did not happen.

Instead this man wanted to get well no matter what it might cost him. He instantly let go of his excuses, his past, and the identity tied to his condition, and he stood on his own feet. He picked up his mat and took that first step and then another and another. In doing so, he broke the cycle of dependency that had left him lying continually on the edge of a miracle but never in its embrace.

ANSWER IN OBEDIENCE

In this amazing scene we witness a paradigm for moving from dependency and paralysis to independence and mobility. The paralyzed man had accepted he would likely never get healed—after all, he did not even ask Jesus to help lift him up and carry him into the pool. This man assumed he could never do what needed to be done, never attain what he seemingly longed for so very much. Year after year this man sank deeper and deeper into a mire of emotions: fear, self-pity, hopelessness, and despair.

He depended on others for his breakthrough.

He depended on others for his healing.

He depended on others for his miracle.

But then he encountered Jesus!

When you depend on others more than you depend on God, you will never see the fullness of what God purposed for you. When you depend on others more than you depend on God, perpetual paralysis will define you. When you depend on your weaknesses to define you or your successes to fulfill you, then you paralyze yourself at the edge of the miracle God has for you.

For too long we have depended on others to make us happy.

We have depended on others to make us complete.

We have depended on others for our breakthroughs.

We have depended on government, on the media, and on popular culture to teach our children right and wrong.

We have depended on social media to help us define ourselves the way we want others to see us.

We have depended on settling for less than God's best rather than trusting Him for the miracle we need to experience healing.

The time has come for change! The time has come to hear the voice of Jesus asking, "Do you want to get well?" And the time has come to answer Him with your obedience.

Your destiny does not rest in someone else's hands.

Your future does not rest in someone else's hands.

Your family does not rest in someone else's hands.

Your destiny, future, and family rest in the hands of the One who loves you, saves you, redeems you, and heals you. Jesus said, "No one will snatch them out of my hand" (John 10:28). My friend, the time has come to let go of your excuses, move beyond your conditional living, and break your cycle of dependency.

The time has come to stand!

The time has come to step out in faith!

Have you been waiting all your life for your turn to be healed?

You are next!

Chapter Two

YOU ARE NEXT...

TO PUT AN END TO
GENERATIONAL PARALYSIS

You are what you tolerate.

MY PHONE RANG for the third consecutive time in ten minutes, and I took a deep breath before answering. Yet another journalist called to solicit my opinion on the immigration crisis at our country's southern border. The situation commanded everyone's attention, regardless of political affiliation.

As the president of the largest association of Hispanic pastors and Christian leaders in our country, I found my point of view carried weight with media sources eager to quote leaders with a uniquely personal and professional perspective. I did not have answers or instant solutions. I did not criticize our president or give them the sensational sound bites they might have wanted, but I did not want to miss an opportunity to speak on an urgent issue of grave importance.

The irony of the situation had not been lost on me. As an American born in New Jersey and raised in the Lehigh Valley of Pennsylvania, in an area between Philadelphia and Allentown, I could not help but feel just as American as anyone else in our working-class, suburban neighborhood. Yet in middle school I faced bullying from other students for being of Puerto Rican descent. Sadly enough I also encountered prejudice from some of the adults. I will never forget the shock and anger I felt while sitting in the guidance counselor's office as a high school freshman. We had scheduled a meeting to discuss my course selections, which at that time tended to tilt toward college and a professional career or else toward skilled labor as part of a blue-collar workforce.

When the counselor asked what I thought about my future, I told her of my interest in computers and computer engineering.

She did not take it seriously and patronized me as a nerdy kid with no idea how the world works, directing me toward construction, landscaping, or some other trade labor. It meant nothing to her that I had a high grade point average and took honors courses that placed me near the top of my large class. This woman could not imagine me as a college-educated professional. Bless her heart, she probably thought she did me a favor! But my encounter that day motivated me to work even harder to show her, and everyone like her, that I would never be paralyzed because of demographic or generational factors.

POLITICAL PARALYSIS

Whether my voice influenced long-lasting solutions to the issues surrounding our country's policies on immigration, I do not know. But I do know the problems within our country—on this volatile issue and so many more—can either unite us, making us stronger as we overcome obstacles together, or continue to divide us, splintering us into factions and paralyzing us to the point where our problems feel insurmountable. I am a firm believer that obstacles represent opportunities in disguise.

With issues such as immigration I am keenly reminded, however, that cultural, social, and political obstacles can also paralyze us, both as individuals and as a nation, if we wait on someone else to do something. Like the man at the pool of Bethesda we can wait on someone else to put an end to the generational paralysis we have inherited, or we can listen to the voice of Jesus and experience freedom from a legacy of loss as we find healing and discover our divine destiny.

The choice is ours.

And it starts with you and me.

Right here and right now.

Obviously I believe our country and our world can only find hope in Jesus Christ. And this hope spreads and makes a difference in overcoming the shackles of prejudice, poverty, and paralysis through the local Christian church. God calls you and I, along with the millions of other followers of Jesus united within the church around the world, to be His bearers of light in a world that seems to grow dimmer each day.

And the fact that so many reporters, journalists, and media anchors wanted to interview me on the topic of immigration highlights that the perceived separation of church and state does not apply when it comes to matters of human life and moral integrity. As people committed to following Christ's example, we of all people should be willing to act, to serve, and to lead. I fear that instead we succumb to the generational paralysis afflicting us like an epidemic.

> **We do not need more followers of the donkey or the elephant. Our nation needs more followers of the Lamb!**

You only need to turn on your phone, laptop, tablet, or flat screen and scroll to a news source. Turn on Fox, MSNBC, CNN, ABC, NBC, CBS, or even Univision, and you will see our country's paralysis. Political correctness paralyzes us. Political discord renders us powerless. Economic disparity disables us. Lack of communication impairs us. An attitude of distrust toward those who are different incapacitates us.

An unwillingness to respect those with whom we disagree freezes us in our tracks.

Does anyone have the answer? Before you begin to wonder if I am running for political office—I am not! Please understand that I am not complaining. We do not need more followers of the donkey or the elephant. Our nation needs more followers of the Lamb!

The answer to America's paralysis is Jesus.

The answer to America's paralysis is the church of Jesus Christ!

Not just any church but a united church. A divided church will never heal a broken nation. The answer to our nation's paralysis is a holy church (1 Pet. 1:16), a healed church (1 Pet. 2:24), a healthy church (3 John 2), and a happy church (John 15:11)! But to change the church, the nation, and the world, we must first confront our own personal paralysis. For at the end of the day Uncle Sam may be our uncle, but he will never be our heavenly Father.

LIFE INTRUDES

We all suffer from paralysis at various times in our lives. Our immobility may be the result of a devastating injury, a debilitating illness, or a dangerous addiction. We may be stuck in place because of someone else's betrayal. We may be frozen by fears of what might happen if we risk stepping out in faith as God calls us. We might cling to false beliefs about our identity based on our circumstances, our family of origin, and our limitations.

But consider how many times in the Bible individuals paralyzed by indecision, inaction, and inconsistency are energized
into action by the power of God. When God wants to use
us, nothing and no one can limit Him! Ironically, too often
we limit Him because we look with our mortal eyes. One of
my favorite "movers" in the faith is Abram, who went on to
become Abraham.

Stops and starts characterize his entire story. Our first
introduction to Abram comes as he moves with his father
from Ur to Canaan: "Terah took his son Abram, his grandson
Lot son of Haran, and his daughter-in-law Sarai, the wife of
his son Abram, and together they set out from Ur of the
Chaldeans to go to Canaan. But when they came to Harran,
they settled there. Terah lived 205 years, and he died in
Harran" (Gen. 11:31–32).

Now the Chaldeans in the land of Ur worshipped idols, not
the living God who prompted Terah to move to Canaan, the
land later known as the Promised Land because God promised
it to Abram and guided the people of Israel there after deliv-
ering them from slavery in Egypt. And while God called Terah
as well as Abram, for some reason Terah never made it to the
destination God had for him. Maybe he grew tired or became
sick and could not travel any farther. We do not know.

But we do know that Terah settled in Harran and died there.
He did not finish the journey he started. He stalled out and
ended up dying between where he started and where God
wanted to take him. You and I both have seen the same situation occur over and over again with people we know today.
They start out strong in pursuit of their God-given dreams and
cannot wait to follow Him to their own promised land.

But then life intrudes.

Most likely you have experienced it in your own life as well.

The college degree you worked so hard to attain has not helped you find a job in your field—but your student loans have come due nonetheless. The plumbing backs up in the house and the repair requires thousands of dollars you do not have. The spouse you committed your love to for the rest of your life betrays your vows and decides to divorce you. The children who used to be scared of the dark and run to you for comfort now face the darkness of addiction and run away from the help you offer. The body that has always been strong and healthy suddenly fails you, unable to bear the chronic pain that years of stress has produced.

In the midst of life's intrusions we lose sight of our dreams. We get stuck and do not know how to keep going. We settle for less than God's best and do whatever it takes just to get by for another day. We accept Harran instead of pressing on for Canaan. We feel foolish for ever thinking that we could have made it to such a lofty destination. We feel ashamed for losing hope in God's ability to get us unstuck. We feel angry that others seem to pass us by and see their dreams realized while we remain left behind.

And when you settle for Harran instead of Canaan, your children will likely settle there too. Perhaps you saw what your parents worked so hard to attain slip through their fingers during the economic recession or when Alzheimer's claimed their minds. Maybe they never finished college and could not help you get your education either. Perhaps your parents divorced and sent the message that marriages do not last.

I have a revelation for you: we all suffer from paralysis—perhaps not physical but spiritual, emotional, financial, or relational. You find yourself reading this even as you struggle to move forward in your life. You have lost your mobility and your motivation for taking action. Disappointed by other people, circumstances, and the consequences of your own choices, you struggle with paralyzed dreams.

Paralyzed integrity.

Paralyzed faith.

Paralyzed destiny.

Paralyzed career.

Paralyzed relationships.

Paralyzed ministries.

So many factors can deaden the nerves in our soul to the point where we lose feeling. We lose our sense of spiritual balance and our ability to trust God as we step out in faith. Many things plague us: sin, failure, fear, the past, shame, religious condemnation, self-pity, victimization, poverty, abuse, broken relationships, unforgiveness, and unbelief. We are paralyzed.

Paralyzed by others' opinions of us.

Paralyzed by what others say about us.

Paralyzed by the constant need to be affirmed and validated.

Paralyzed by fear—both what we see in the outside world and what we see when we look inside our own heart.

Just like that man by the pool at Bethesda, at a corporate macro level generations are paralyzed in North America and around the world, crippled by moral relativism, cultural decadence, spiritual apathy, violence, corruption, darkness, hatred, bigotry, intolerance, perversion, and death.

THE IDENTITY OF THE BELIEVER

The enemy of grace, truth, and love desires to paralyze your future through definitions, nomenclatures, and descriptors assigned to you that do not line up with God's prophetic destiny and purpose for you. In other words, the enemy will paralyze you if you do not have certainty about your identity in Christ! Therefore, you must ask yourself these critical questions:

> Who am I?
> Am I defined by my past?
> Am I defined by my circumstances?
> Am I defined by what people say about me?

I have great news from what took place on the cross: Christ defines you.

> The things that surround you do not define you.
> *God's Spirit inside of you defines you.*

> Your circumstances do not define you.
> *His covenant defines you.*

> The hell you are going through does not define you.
> *The heaven you are going to defines you.*

> Your failures do not define you.
> *His forgiveness defines you.*

For all my Facebook, Twitter, and Instagram brothers and sisters:

The likes of many do not define you.
The love of One defines you.

And for all the religious folk:

What you do for God does not define you.
What God already did for you—through the cross, empty
tomb, Upper Room, His blood, and His Word—defines
you!

The Father defines you.
The Son defines you.
The Holy Spirit defines you.
Galatians 2:20 defines you: "I have been crucified with Christ
and I no longer live, but Christ lives in me. The life I now live
in the body, I live by faith in the Son of God, who loved me and
gave himself for me."

THE IDENTITY OF THE BODY OF CHRIST

With so many attempting to define us as the body of Christ, it
behooves us to ask ourselves the same questions collectively:

Who are we as Christ followers?
Who are we as His church?
Are we just another institution in society?
Are we another religious faith narrative competing in the
marketplace of ideas?
Are we a feel-good device for the spiritually impaired?

Are we an antiquated conduit of irrelevant values no longer applicable in the world of Facebook, Twitter, Instagram, and YouTube?

Our response will determine whether light will overcome darkness in our generation. So who are we? With clarity, conviction, and courage we must give the following response:

We are the light of the world.
We are a city on a hill.
We are people of the Word.
We are salt and light.
We are prophetic and not pathetic.
We are disciples, witnesses, and Christ followers.
We are evangelists, pastors, and teachers.
We are children of the cross, fruit of the empty tomb, and
a product of the Upper Room.
We are the redeemed of the Lord.
We are the sheep of His pasture.
We are forgiven, free, and favored.
We are called and chosen.
We are warriors and worshippers.
We are the righteousness of God.
We are world changers and history makers.

Let me also tell you what we are *not*. We are not Google, Microsoft, Ford, or even Starbucks. We are the church of Jesus Christ, and the gates of hell shall not, cannot, and will not prevail against us! Hallelujah!

Now that you have answered the question of your identity, you must next answer the voice of Jesus calling out: "Do you want to get well?"

THE EDGE OF POSSIBILITY

We all want to get well. No one likes being paralyzed. I cannot imagine anyone choosing to remain paralyzed when presented with the opportunity to be healed and whole again. But sometimes the risk, the fear, and the uncertainty of answering Jesus' call seem too overpowering. It seems easier, safer, and more convenient to stay on the ground, wishing someone else could help you get to the water while accepting that you can never get there fast enough. Resigning yourself to a lifetime of paralysis, while devastating and immobilizing, strangely enough seems preferable to standing up and daring to take that first step.

Paralysis, however, comes in part from being caught between immobility and possibility. Maybe you have been told to accept that your situation will never change. But once you glimpse the possibility for a miracle, how can you close the door of your heart's belief in healing? No matter how much your mind tries to insist a miracle will not happen, you begin asking yourself, "What if?"

What if healing could somehow be within reach? You think your marriage might be over, but what if a miracle happened and you and your spouse forgave each other and restored your relationship? You talk to the bill collectors and assume you will have to declare bankruptcy, but what if you found money you did not know you had and could pay off your debts? You presume you will never be promoted at work because you do not have a degree, but what if your supervisor noticed your hard work and rewarded you with a raise?

The paralyzed man knew what it means to wonder, "What if?" and wait and wait and wait for something to change. Even if he had resigned himself to paralysis, he nonetheless remained there beside the pool. He stayed at the edge of possibility, hoping against hope that somehow, some way, he might make it into the rippled waters first. As slow as he was, he knew cognitively, rationally, and logically that he would never be the first to make it into the pool after the angel stirred the water.

Yet he did not leave.

He stayed there even when it did not make much sense.

Sometimes we can only stay at the edge of possibility, hoping with no logical reason for a solution, a change, a healing. We cannot see a way forward. We have forgotten what it feels like to stand and walk on our own. We feel sorry for ourselves and resent that others receive the healing we long to experience.

Yet we cling to hope at the edge of possibility.

JUST DO IT

Other days we find it too painful to hope for more, too scary to think about what life might have been like if we had gotten what we have been needing for years and years. Because then we might not know who to be and how to live. We get so used to being paralyzed that we cannot imagine who we would be if we could walk again.

We know if we stand and try to take that step in our own power, we might fall down and be right back where we started. We might even feel shame at the thought of trying again after struggling and straining to get on our feet only to collapse yet again. At first our anger might propel us to keep trying and then try harder, but eventually we become so exhausted that our willpower runs out.

Think about your own life for a moment. Think about those specific areas where you feel numb and unable to move forward. Think about the dreams that have withered and left you feeling like a victim of atrophied hope.

How many times have you tried to work harder and do better? How often do you promise yourself you will go back and finish that degree, stand up to your boss, or look for a new job? How many times have you tried to give up an abusive relationship only to fail? How many times a day do you criticize yourself for overeating, smoking, spending too much time online, or drinking too much?

> We often feel like victims because we cannot overcome our paralysis by ourselves. But God never intended for us to do it on our own.

You can never overcome your personal, generational paralysis in your own power. Writing to the community of believers in Rome, Paul explained, "I do not understand what I do. For what I want to do I do not do, but what I hate I do....For I have the desire to do what is good, but I cannot carry it out" (Rom. 7:15, 18). When have you felt powerless to do what you knew God wanted you to do? When have you wrestled with temptation only to succumb to the enemy's attacks and end up doing what you know you do not want to do?

The good news—no, the *absolutely great* news—is that you do not have to rely on your own power. Paul concluded, "What a wretched man I am! Who will rescue me from this body that is subject to death? Thanks be to God, who delivers me through Jesus Christ our Lord!" (Rom. 7:24–25). We often feel like victims because we cannot overcome our paralysis by ourselves. But God never intended for us to do it on our own. So He sent His Son to die for our sins, and He sent the Holy Spirit to live in our hearts.

You do not need to be a victim, my friend! God has given you the victory through your relationship with His Son, Jesus Christ. When Jesus told the paralyzed man to walk, the man picked up his mat and walked. When God calls you to move, it does not matter who your parents are and what they did or did not do. Like the paralyzed man, you just have to do it—not think about it, talk about it, or analyze it. Long before the phrase became synonymous with Nike, the message came from the voice of Jesus as He told a man to get up and walk.

Just do it.

MAKE A BREAK

I know it seems too simple to be true. You want to just do it, but everyone around you reminding you of your paralysis makes it tough. And you tend to believe them because you find it too painful to hope for more. Especially when those voices belong to your parents, it can seem impossible to break free and do what you have never seen them do.

But you are not your parents.

Your life does not have to turn out the same way theirs did. Your marriage does not have to end just because theirs did. You do not have to struggle with addiction to prescription painkillers just because they did. You do not have to give up hope and sink into depression just because they did. They may have settled for Harran instead of Canaan, but you do not have to stay where they were. You can bury them and their paralysis and move on!

So often we want to blame our parents for our paralysis, but God tears down that excuse. Yes, our mothers and fathers dramatically influence our lives. So do our grandparents, guardians, and even the caretakers we knew while we were children. But their mistakes do not determine our lives! We may suffer the consequences of their bad choices and wrong decisions, but they do not have the power to render us paralyzed for the rest of our lives. We can make a break with generational paralysis and allow Jesus to make us whole.

Jesus pointed this out to His followers when faced with healing a man who could not see. As Christ walked with His disciples, they came upon a man who had been blind since birth. The disciples asked their Master whether the man's own sins or the sins of his parents had caused his blindness. The Lord's answer surprised them: "'Neither this man nor his parents sinned,' said Jesus, 'but this happened so that the works of God might be displayed in him'" (John 9:3). Jesus meant that the man had been freed from the curse of the Law because it put demands on people that no one could keep.

In today's vernacular we would call this news a game changer for people accustomed to being stuck in life based on the family into which they were born. Under the Law God gave to Moses, the sins of the father often echoed throughout the generations that followed. But when Jesus came and died on the cross for our sins, He forever broke the power of any curses, strongholds, or generational sin. The Bible tells us, "Christ redeemed us from the curse of the law by becoming a curse for us, for it is written: 'Cursed is everyone who is hung on a pole.' He redeemed us in order that the blessing given to Abraham might come to the Gentiles through Christ Jesus, so that by faith we might receive the promise of the Spirit" (Gal. 3:13–14).

Do you know what this means? The promised land awaits you!

No matter where your parents, grandparents, or ancestors settled before reaching the promised land, that place no longer holds you. The "blessing given to Abraham" mentioned in this passage from Galatians draws us back to an example we must not overlook. Because you see, after his father died in Harran, God spoke to Abram and reminded him that the time to move on had come.

> Go from your country, your people and your father's household to the land I will show you. I will make you into a great nation, and I will bless you; I will make your name great, and you will be a blessing. I will bless those who bless you, and whoever curses you I will curse; and all peoples on earth will be blessed through you.
> —GENESIS 12:1–3

This blessing, so Galatians 3:13–14 tells us, belongs not just to the Jewish people as direct descendants of Abraham but to the Gentiles as well. What Jesus did for all people sets you and me free from any forces of the past attempting to paralyze us.

WALKING IN FREEDOM

You might be aware of areas of paralysis in your life as you struggle to believe God can release you from the generational weight that continues to pin you down. Perhaps you think, "I know God can heal me, Pastor Sam, but I am tired of waiting and hoping. I have too much to overcome. Even if I get on my feet, I will always limp along."

While I understand this feeling, I must challenge you to let go of the chains that bind you and to walk in the freedom you have in Christ instead. Jesus said, "The Spirit of the Lord is on me, because he has anointed me to proclaim good news to the poor. He has sent me to proclaim freedom for the prisoners and recovery of sight for the blind, to set the oppressed free" (Luke 4:18). You have been set free, my friend, no matter what chains may have shackled you or what generational consequences you may have inherited.

The tricky part is now walking in your new freedom. You may have heard about caged animals that grow so used to the comfort and familiarity of their confinement that even when people set them free to return to the wild, they stay put. These wild creatures made to live in jungles, rainforests, and woods have grown accustomed to seeing bars in front of them. They can now leave their prisons behind and walk through the open doors of their cages. But that means stepping out into the unknown wilderness.

Perhaps, like a caged animal set free, you feel apprehensive about who you would be and what your life would become if you got on your feet and began walking in the power of God. Take a moment and ask yourself, "Who would I be if I had the peace and security I have always longed to have? Who would I be if I trusted God to provide for my every need and rested in the knowledge of His sovereignty? Who would I be if I stopped blaming my parents, my kids, my abuser, my boss, my in-laws, and my enemies?"

As a runner I know how daunting it can be to look at the finish line miles down the road and wonder how I will ever get there. As a leader I know how overwhelming it can be to look at what needs to happen for change to take place in our communities. As a pastor I know how intimidating it can be to serve those who feel broken, hopeless, and desperate. Left to my own abilities, I would remain afraid, overwhelmed, and intimidated. But then I hear the voice of Jesus telling me to get up and walk!

GOD CONQUERS. YOU POSSESS. YOUR CHILDREN INHERIT.

So Joshua called together the twelve men he had chosen—one from each of the tribes of Israel. He told them, "Go into the middle of the Jordan, in front of the Ark of the LORD your God. Each of you must pick up one stone and carry it out on your shoulder—twelve stones in all, one for each of the twelve tribes of Israel. We will use these stones to build a memorial. In the future your children will ask you, 'What do these stones mean?' Then you can tell them, 'They remind us that the Jordan River stopped flowing when the Ark of the Lord's Covenant went across.' These stones will stand as a memorial among the people of Israel forever."

—Joshua 4:4–7, nlt

God tells them...

When I take you across, build something.

When I give you the victory, build something.

When I get you to the other side, build something.

Not for your sake, but for the sake of your children and your children's children, those who follow you.

More than ever I hear the Spirit say, "What I am doing is not just for you; it's more about your children and your children's children." Because as it pertains to fulfilling destiny and advancing God's kingdom in Jesus' name:

God conquers.

You possess.

Your children inherit.

This is why the battle is so intense. This is why darkness prevails. This is why the kingdom suffers violence. Because it's not just about you! It's about the Father above you, Jesus in front of you, the Spirit inside of you, and your children who follow you! So when you get your breakthrough, build. When you cross, construct. But not for your sake!

Build something—for them!

Cross—for them!

Don't give up—for them!

Then as I looked over the situation, I called together the nobles and the rest of the people and said to them, "Don't

be afraid of the enemy! Remember the Lord, who is great
and glorious, and fight for your brothers, your sons, your
daughters, your wives."

—NEHEMIAH 4:14, NLT

This means there are times God picked you up, not for your
sake but for them. There are times you failed, sinned, went
down, or turned from God, but God had mercy, not just for
your sake but for them!

When God took you out...

When God picked you up...

When God cleaned you off...

When God redeemed, repaired, and restored you, He did not
do it just for you—He also did it for them!

So why build a memorial? Why an altar? Because God wants
you to tell them! Share the story! I know we grew up believing
that there are certain things we must keep from our kids. I
know the standard modus operandi is to protect our children
from our failures. But with grace as your goal and love as your
guide, tell them what you went through. Tell them what you
faced. Tell them how you overcame by the blood of the Lamb
and word of your testimony!

The greatest inheritance you can give your children is your
testimony. Psalm 119:111 says, "Your testimonies are my heritage forever, for they are the joy of my heart" (ESV). Stop trying
to hide what God wants you to share. Tell them your story.

Once upon a time...

But God...

Instead of...

"This is my story, this is my song."[1]

Each generation will announce to the next your wonderful and powerful deeds.

—Psalm 145:4, cev

What you have done will be praised from one generation to the next; they will proclaim your mighty acts.

—Psalm 145:4, gnt

So the people of Israel built an altar, a memorial, a testimony! And we do the same. Each stone is something that you overcame.

This is where God showed up.

This is where God broke my chains.

This is where addiction died.

This is where captivity was taken captive.

This is where fear fled.

Remember, God conquers. You possess. Your children inherit. And what does the inheritance of your children look like?

Your children will come home!

He will turn the hearts of the parents to their children, and the hearts of the children to their parents.

—Malachi 4:6

But now this is what the Lord says: "Do not weep any longer, for I will reward you," says the Lord. "Your children will come back to you from the distant land of the enemy."

—Jeremiah 31:16, nlt

Your children will be saved!

Believe in the Lord Jesus and you will be saved, along with everyone in your household.

—ACTS 16:31, NLT

Your children will prophesy and see what others cannot!

"In the last days," God says, "I will pour out my Spirit upon all people. Your sons and daughters will prophesy. Your young men will see visions, and your old men will dream dreams."

—ACTS 2:17

Your children will never live in what God took you out of!

The two men said to Lot, "Do you have anyone else here…sons or daughters, or anyone else in the city who belongs to you? Get them out of here, because we are going to destroy this place."

—GENESIS 19:12–13

Your children will do greater things!

Very truly I tell you, whoever believes in me will do the works I have been doing, and they will do even greater things than these, because I am going to the Father. And I will do whatever you ask in my name, so that the Father may be glorified in the Son. You may ask me for anything in my name, and I will do it.

—JOHN 14:12–14

For at the end of the day God conquers, you possess, and your children inherit!

God calls each of us to take responsibility for our own lives. He surely wants to use us in the world to influence the lives of others and draw them to the same healing power they see manifest in our own. As Jesus explained while healing the blind man, He reveals His glory and power by doing the impossible in our lives. Perhaps we should recall the words of Edward Everett Hale, "I am only one, but still I am one. I cannot do everything, but still I can do something; and because I cannot do everything, I will not refuse to do the something that I can do."[2]

Will you continue to writhe on the generational ground of past paralysis?

Or will you stand and walk?

You have the choice.

You are next!

Chapter Three

YOU ARE NEXT...

AND THIS TIME YOU WILL NOT MISS YOUR TURN

Truth must never be sacrificed
on the altar of expediency.

SOME YEARS BACK I received a call from a national news source, an iconic pillar of journalistic prominence recognized around the world, asking me for an interview. More than just an interview or sound bite, this media agency wanted to feature me prominently, front and center, in a full-length profile highlighting my life, ministry, and leadership to illustrate what I describe as a new movement committed to reconciling Billy Graham's message of salvation through Christ with Dr. Martin Luther King Jr.'s march for justice: the Lamb's agenda. Who drives this agenda? The fastest-growing demographic redefining Bible-believing Christianity and evangelicalism in the twenty-first century. Welcome to a multiethnic, multigenerational reformation.

This news source sent a reporter and a photographer to shadow me in Sacramento and on a trip to DC in order to capture a variety of candid pictures and videos of my church and me. It thrilled me to stand in my pulpit that Sunday and share with my congregation, many of whom belong to the Lamb's agenda reformation, about this opportunity to share the Lord's work in us and through us. I introduced our guests and explained how they would be taking pictures and interviewing some of them to get a good feel for our church. I tried not to boast but explained how I would be the cover and centerpiece for this major news source's big story.

The next day I engaged in a lengthy conversation with the reporter. While we had enjoyed several shorter, casual conversations, the reporter and I met for our formal, in-depth interview. As we began talking, the journalist subtly and then not so subtly started asking challenging questions about my perspective on social and political issues. I had already made it clear that I considered myself a nonpartisan independent, a leader desiring to advance an agenda of righteousness and justice in the name of Jesus, regardless of the party in control. Reinforcing my position, I explained how I had already worked with both President George W. Bush as well as President Barack Obama.

Nonetheless I began to get the distinct impression of the views the reporter held as this individual began to steer our conversation—along with my responses—toward certain beliefs. We reached an impasse when the journalist politely challenged my pro-life position and unshakable advocacy for religious liberty in light of recent Supreme Court decisions. I explained that I made no judgment on women or anyone holding the pro-choice viewpoint but I just could not compromise the Word of God and His gift of new life, regardless of the human circumstances and consequences. Simply stated, in my mission to advance the grace-filled message of Jesus, I stood committed to one defining principle: truth must never be sacrificed on the altar of political expediency.

As we concluded our conversation, the journalist casually asked about other evangelical Latinos the publication might speak with to round out a portrait of me and this emerging movement. I named several leaders, the reporter thanked me, and we wrapped up our time together. I felt uneasy but could not explain why, so I just prayed for God to work through this opportunity however He wanted.

What could go wrong?

This was my turn, right?

WATCHING THE PARADE
PASS YOU BY

A few weeks went by, and I could not wait for the big story to break. I saw some of the photos from the reporter's visit, including the one I assumed would grace the cover of the iconic periodical in which the article would appear. My parents felt so proud and excited for me. My wife and kids shared my joy and the blessing of such coverage for our church and the movement. My congregation celebrated with me, and I began to receive congratulatory calls and emails from friends and pastors in my network and beyond.

Finally, the story broke. And the word *broke* describes it perfectly because my excitement quickly shattered into pieces that I did not like experiencing: disappointment, anger, frustration, shame, and sadness. My picture did not appear on the cover, but a phrase I had used again and again in the conversation with the reporter provided the headline and title of the story. The article itself featured a few quotations from my interview, but the reporter had gone on to interview several of the very people I had recommended and to showcase them just as prominently.

I felt embarrassed as I faced all the people in my life who had anticipated sharing my joy. Most felt confused and chalked it up to the news media trying to appeal to the broadest audience of consumers. I also felt ashamed that perhaps I had let my hunger run ahead of my humility. While it was no sin to want national attention for our organization and the Christian church, let alone what God had done in the lives of so many men, women, and families in our great nation, I knew that my pride experienced a serious blow.

I also knew in my heart that if I had been willing to say what the reporter wanted me to say, then I would have received what I had been promised. I would have gotten my turn. Instead I watched others step into the spotlight at the moment I thought I would be standing there. I missed my turn. It just did not seem fair somehow. I trusted in God's sovereignty, of course, and I knew I could count on Him and His faithfulness. Still, the entire situation stung me with remorse. Why had this happened?

No matter how I rationalized the outcome or how long and often I prayed and trusted my Savior with the situation, I still felt like a little kid forced to watch the parade pass by without him.

I had missed my turn.

MISSING IN ACTION

The story of the man waiting beside the pool of Bethesda has many aspects, but the part that resonates with me the most is the sense of frustration that comes from waiting for one's turn. That man waited years for his turn, wondering, hoping, and dreaming of the moment he got in the pool first, only to face disappointment, anger, and frustration again and again. Over and over he had to witness countless others rush in and emerge with the exuberant joy as their injury, illness, or infirmity miraculously disappeared. Perhaps the paralyzed man wanted to celebrate with them, to be happy for them, but still...

When would it be his turn?

My situation with the interview profile cannot begin to compare to this man who had been paralyzed for thirty-eight years, and yet we all know that feeling. We all have those moments when we expected something good to happen only to see it slip through our fingers. We all know how it feels to wait our turn and miss out at the last moment.

Maybe you missed the promotion you worked so hard to attain, staying long hours and putting in overtime to make sure you went above and beyond the requirements of your role's responsibilities. Your coworkers praised your work ethic, your customers posted the highest ratings possible, and your boss assured you that your time had come. When the new position opened up, everyone chalked it up to a mere formality when you applied. Surely you had the job!

Until you didn't.

The new hire got the job. Or the CEO's nephew. Or someone on your team you were mentoring. It did not make sense. No one seemed to understand it, but you missed your turn.

> **We all have those moments when we expected something good to happen only to see it slip through our fingers.**

Or perhaps you missed out on the person you were waiting on to spend your life with, a man or woman of God who shared your faith, your desire for a family, your values and interests. You met, began to spend more time together, and started falling in love. Both your families approved and could not wait until you tied the knot. As the months passed by, you anticipated the proposal that would formalize what you just knew you had both been feeling.

But it never came.

Your would-be fiancé decided to see someone else, wanting to be friends with you and nothing more. As perfect as you seemed for each other, the love of your life passed you by and left you more alone than ever before. You thought you would be married and soon start a family, but you missed your turn.

Maybe you have struggled with a physical condition your entire life, one that has placed limits on your ability to take pleasure in all the areas of life you see others enjoy. You have learned to compensate, perhaps through medication or devices or the help of others, but you long to live life with both feet on the ground, just as the paralyzed man at Bethesda must have dreamed of for so long. Week after week, month after month, you have done what you know you must do to become stronger—physical therapy, exercise, and a healthy lifestyle. You have seen others with your same condition get well and become whole again, so the possibility cannot be denied.

And yet...it has not happened for you.

You still struggle.

You still try.

Your hope runs out.

You secretly fear being too late.

You have missed your turn.

And that is the way it is.

BACK OF THE LINE

"Dad, she got two cookies, and I only got one!"

"No fair! Mom, he got to stay up later than me!"

"I got here first! They broke line—make them get at the back of the line!"

"When do I get my turn? Everybody else has already had one. I want my turn!"

When our children were young, Eva and I often found ourselves caught in the middle of sorting out situations based on our kids' testimony. As with most little ones, it was not unusual for them to blame each other for broken toys or messy rooms and to feel they deserved to be treated in a superior way to their siblings. They wanted the world to be fair when convenient, but they also wanted everything tilted to their advantage.

As grown-ups we often do the same.

We tend toward the extremes, feeling like a victim of life's unfairness while also feeling entitled to have what we want the way we want it. As we watch others receive the job, the spouse, the family, the career, the health, or the material blessings we so long to enjoy, we grow weary of waiting. We cannot understand why others get what we want while we continue to suffer and struggle, waiting and watching.

We cannot fathom why someone else always gets there ahead of us. We feel owed, entitled, and promised, and we just cannot come to terms with why we remain stuck in place, paralyzed by so much responsibility, so many bills, so little money, and so much work yet to be done.

Sometimes when we miss our turn, it feels especially painful because we have never stopped keeping our faith. We know that God is good and sovereign. Surely He wants the best for us, right? God's Word assures us, "And we know that in all things God works for the good of those who love him, who have been called according to his purpose" (Rom. 8:28). So why has He not answered our prayers, healed our wounds, or restored our relationships? We think, "If God loves me—and I know He does—then why have I not had my turn?"

We get tired of waiting.

Our patience wears thin.

We decide to take matters into our own hands.

TAKING OUR TURN

We need to remember, of course, that our idea of best might differ greatly from God's knowledge of best, according to His divine wisdom and omniscience. God's ways are higher than our ways, and we cannot know all that He knows. As spiritual beings in mortal bodies, we have a limited grasp through our senses and our intellect, as well as by the confinement of linear time as we know it. Our best often falls far short of the eternal best that God wants to pour into our lives.

Even when God gives us personal assurance or a prophetic insight, we may not get what we feel He has promised us in the way we expected. Those situations often tempt us to take matters into our own hands and try to force people and events to conform to what we believe we—and God—want to be done. God wants us to wait on Him and remain patient in the face of obstacles and impossible odds. But we want to hit the fast-forward button and jump to the healing, the miracle, the promise fulfilled, and the gift.

One of the most intriguing examples emerges from the life of Jacob, whom God later renamed Israel, the founding father of God's nation of Jewish people. I find it striking though that even before Jacob came along, God promised Jacob's grandfather, Abraham, that he would be the beginning of a mighty nation of people that would endure for all time. Who would not be overjoyed to receive such a promise from the Lord?

But the years turned into a decade, and still Abraham and his wife, Sarah, had not conceived a child together. They had grown older, and Sarah was not physically be able to become pregnant. The two of them then tried to force the situation, with Sarah offering her maid, Hagar, to be a kind of surrogate mother to birth Abraham an heir, which she did. (Read Genesis 16 for the full story.)

Only God did not have that in mind. God intended to give Abraham and Sarah a son, and so He did. Sarah gave birth to a baby boy they named Isaac, which means laughter. I suspect these two old parents felt so overjoyed at doing the impossible, conceiving and bearing a son in their old age, that they could not stop laughing.

Isaac grew up and fathered two sons of his own, twin boys Esau and Jacob. Even before they were born, God indicated that Jacob, the younger likely by a matter of minutes, would rule over his older brother, Esau, the firstborn. Notice how the characters of these two caused them both to feel like they had missed their turn.

> Isaac prayed to the LORD on behalf of his wife, because she was childless. The LORD answered his prayer, and his wife Rebekah became pregnant. The babies jostled each other within her, and she said, "Why is this happening to me?" So she went to inquire of the LORD.
>
> The LORD said to her, "Two nations are in your womb, and two peoples from within you will be separated; one people will be stronger than the other, and the older will serve the younger."

... The boys grew up, and Esau became a skillful hunter, a man of the open country, while Jacob was content to stay at home among the tents. Isaac, who had a taste for wild game, loved Esau, but Rebekah loved Jacob. Once when Jacob was cooking some stew, Esau came in from the open country, famished. He said to Jacob, "Quick, let me have some of that red stew! I am famished!" (That is why he was also called Edom.)

Jacob replied, "First sell me your birthright."

"Look, I am about to die," Esau said. "What good is the birthright to me?"

But Jacob said, "Swear to me first." So he swore an oath to him, selling his birthright to Jacob. Then Jacob gave Esau some bread and some lentil stew. He ate and drank, and then got up and left. So Esau despised his birthright.

—Genesis 25:21–23, 27–34

The story does not end there, though, because Jacob secured the other dimension of his identity as the most significant son. With his mother's help Jacob pretended to be his brother, Esau, and brought food to his father. The old man, unable to see well and fooled by the animal skins Jacob wore to mimic his brother's hairy forearms, then blessed the trickster with the traditional blessing a father could only give to his firstborn son.

Jacob got what he wanted—so he thought. Except that his life got worse instead of better for many years. The guilt of tricking his father likely weighed on him. The shame of exploiting his brother and stealing his inheritance just added to the crushing weight Jacob carried. Ironically, of course, by working so hard to achieve what Jacob believed God had promised him before birth, Jacob set in motion consequences that only caused more chaos, heartache, and deception for everyone in his family.

Jacob thought he missed his turn, so he did something about it. He did not get what he bargained for in return. Once again he must have felt disappointed. Jacob kept running, afraid of facing his brother. He got married—twice, in fact—grew wealthy, and the Lord blessed him, but Jacob knew things were not right.

He still missed out on what he most desired.

NEVER ENOUGH

Jacob's story reminds us that even when we have attained what we thought we wanted, it does not equate to waiting on what God has for us. After all of his running, after all of his waiting and waiting, Jacob finally had more than he could have hoped for. By most of his neighbors' standards, Isaac's youngest son had become a rich man: two wives, a dozen sons, large flocks, and countless goats and donkeys. These insufficient attempts at compensation could not stop the past from haunting him.

We cannot excuse or justify what Jacob did. Rather than waiting on the Lord's timing, he stole his twin brother's birthright by conspiring with their mother, Rebekah, and outright deceiving and lying to their father, Isaac. Jacob also took advantage of Esau by exploiting a situation in which Jacob found his brother famished after a long hunting trip. Knowing his scam would be discovered, Jacob ran and kept running for much of his life.

At first he went to live with his Uncle Laban, where Jacob experienced a similar kind of duplicity and exploitation that he himself had perpetrated previously on his own family. After enduring seven years of labor necessary to marry Rachel, the woman he loved, Laban tricked Jacob into marrying her sister, Leah. He then had to work seven more years, which he did, to wed Rachel. But even then Jacob still had not found the peace of knowing his turn had come.

Born into situations beyond our control, we might be tempted to blame our parents, our families, and the limitations of our socioeconomic boundaries. We may resign ourselves to believing that we can never rise above the baseline of our birth. Or we may work hard to better ourselves and achieve what we consider to be what we deserve. Yet even after we appear successful by the world's standards, we still feel cheated, still feel shortchanged, still feel deprived of the peace, purpose, and passion we see others enjoying.

I suspect that even from birth Jacob likely felt like he had missed his turn, grabbing his brother's heel as they raced out of the womb and into the world. Thus, his very name, Jacob, meaning heel-catcher or supplanter, reflected the fact that he missed his turn and did not emerge as the firstborn, who traditionally received the father's blessing and the birthright to inherit most of his father's wealth.

In the Bible, names often reflect one's character or personality. We cannot know if Jacob naturally was a trickster, chaser, or con man at heart or if he grew into his name because others expected it of him. Regardless, he seems to have lived up—or down, as the case may be—to what his name implied about him: someone always running after his turn, chasing the next opportunity to finally get what he needed to be whole.

> You must remember your true identity in Christ. He did not make you a runner-up, second-best, too-late person who missed a divine appointment with destiny.

Sometimes when you miss your turn, you struggle to get over it. You feel cheated. You might grow angry at God and, like Jacob, decide to take matters into your own hands, determined that you will take what should be yours since you missed your turn. Whether intentionally or inadvertently, you step on other people, ignore the consequences, and demand the blessing that passed you by. Perhaps you cut corners at work in order to take more money home. Maybe you omit the truth with your family to get what you want from them. Whatever the circumstances, you compromise your integrity to attain what you believe will satisfy your soul.

However, if you desire to experience the same healing and walk by faith, as the man by the pool in Bethesda did, you must remember your true identity in Christ. He did not make you a runner-up, second-best, too-late person who missed a divine appointment with destiny. He made you a son or daughter of the King! And although you might seemingly miss an opportunity or watch someone else enjoy something you thought was intended for you, God will always bless you with what you truly need!

The man at Bethesda thought he needed someone to help him get in the pool. He believed he needed to be just a little quicker, a little more responsive to receive the healing he so desperately wanted. But as it turned out, he did not need either of these ingredients! He simply needed Jesus.

FIGHTING FOR YOUR FAITH

You might know you need Jesus, and you might already know Him as your Lord and Savior. Maybe you have been waiting a long, long time for your turn. Whatever you do now, my friend, do not give up! God has not brought you this far to abandon you now—He has promised never to leave or forsake you! What if your turn awaits this afternoon, tonight, tomorrow, this weekend, or next month? Trust that God has a blessing waiting on you just around the corner. Believe that your turn has come!

Jacob dreaded having a showdown with his angry brother, Esau. Decades had passed since they had last spoken or seen each other. But Jacob knew he had to finally face up to the follies of his past mistakes if he wanted to receive the spiritual inheritance God had promised him. Jacob mustered his courage and showed up to square off against his brother—only Esau did not show up.

Instead Jacob found himself face to face with himself. He sent his wives, servants, and children away and put down his defenses. Alone, Jacob wrestled with God in the guise of a man and refused to give up until God blessed him.

> So Jacob was left alone, and a man wrestled with him till daybreak. When the man saw that he could not over-power him, he touched the socket of Jacob's hip so that his hip was wrenched as he wrestled with the man. Then the man said, "Let me go, for it is daybreak."
>
> But Jacob replied, "I will not let you go unless you bless me."
>
> The man asked him, "What is your name?"
>
> "Jacob," he answered.
>
> Then the man said, "Your name will no longer be Jacob, but Israel, because you have struggled with God and with humans and have overcome."
>
> —Genesis 32:24–28

Jacob's turn had finally arrived. He refused to give up! He could no longer run, no longer hide, no longer strive. Jacob stopped chasing after all the pursuits he believed would compensate for not having the turn he thought he deserved. And when Jacob stopped running, he came face to face with God. Wrestling and refusing to give in or give up, Jacob received God's blessing, symbolized by a new name, Israel, and by the limp that would go with him the rest of his life.

Like Jacob, you may feel battered and bruised, limping and struggling to get by. But you do not have to fight any longer. You have persevered and won God's favor. You no longer have to fight for your turn because God wants to bless you.

To receive what the Lord has for you only requires your faith. Faith, and faith alone, saves you. You do not have to solve problems, resolve conflicts, provide solutions, make others change, or force anything to happen.

What if the problem you thought you had is really not the problem?

What if you simply need to stop worrying so much and working so hard and surrender your need at the feet of the Lord Jesus Christ?

What if you are next in line to receive God's best?

YOUR TIME HAS COME

When God shows up in your life, He makes you next even if you missed your turn before! Four years after I missed my turn with the interview profile, I looked out upon hundreds of thousands of people as I stood on the platform only a few feet away from where the inauguration of our new president would take place. I delivered a prayer, seen and heard by millions of people around the world, only moments before our country's new leader took the oath of office. Suddenly calls, texts, and emails bombarded me, asking for interviews, opinions, articles, books, prayers, and anything else I wanted to share!

My turn had come.

I thought I had missed my turn years ago, but God had something even bigger and greater waiting for me. I would never have been standing at the presidential podium addressing millions of people around the world on Inauguration Day in 2017 if I had missed my turn! Looking out at the sea of faces, I marveled—and still do—at what God had done in my life and what He continues to do each and every day. What looked like a missed turn years ago had actually prepared me for something greater.

When Jesus says, "Your turn has come!" one word comes to mind: Wow! By the grace of God (1 Cor. 15:10), the man overlooked years ago has become a presidential adviser, best-selling author, movie producer, megachurch pastor, and above all a grateful beneficiary of the grace of Jesus.

You might think you have missed your turn, but I am writing this book to tell you that your turn has come, my friend. Something bigger, better, and bolder than you expected or imagined will happen soon. Do you think the man beside the pool of Bethesda believed he would ever walk, actually walk, in the manner he did? One moment he has lying there on the ground waiting, wondering, wistfully wishing he could have his turn. And the next moment, Jesus commands him to walk, and he stands to his feet, taking step after step!

Jesus shows up and makes this man, paralyzed for almost forty years, next in line. The man waits on someone to help him get to the edge of the pool in hopes that somehow, some way, he could be the first in the water, no matter how unlikely. Apparently he tried before, but because of his debilitating paralysis he simply moved too slowly. Other people, ambulatory and with full mobility, rush in to splash and bathe in the healing waters, receiving the healing bestowed by being the first.

> You might think you have missed your turn, but I am writing this book to tell you...something bigger, better, and bolder than you expected or imagined will happen soon.

How many times have you expected it to be your turn when in fact it did not end up being your moment after all? How much longer will you wait while the opportunity slips away to grow, change, and be all God made you to be? How can you continue to settle for less than God's best when Jesus stands right before you asking, "Do you want to get well?"

You have been waiting for your turn.
You have been praying for your turn.
You have been fasting for your turn.
You have been hoping for your turn.
You have been through hell for your turn.

You have fought off devils, demons, principalities, powers of darkness, strangers, family, and even yourself for your turn! And just like the man beside the pool at Bethesda, you have asked, "When will I be next?"

I am telling you in the name of Jesus that because of what you have been through, because of where you will go—not just for your sake, but for the sake of your children and your children's children—the time to walk by faith has come. Stop waiting on someone else to heal you, help you, or hand you the divine destiny God has for you. No longer will you sit on the sidelines and watch others rush to receive the bounty of blessings that belong to you. You have finished being paralyzed by fear, by anger, by disappointment, or by circumstances.

Don't miss this moment!

Put a smile on your face, a praise on your lips, and a twinkle in your eyes because, ready or not, you are next! I do not merely pray or hope this for you, my friend; I believe God promises it to you! Who can stop what God has purposed (Isa. 14:27)? He declares, "At the right time, I, the LORD, will make it happen" (Isa. 60:22, NLT). I dare you to believe with me that you are next!

You may have missed your turn before but not this time. This time you are next in line! No one will cut in front of you. No one else will receive what God wants to give you. No one else can ever steal what has been eternally purposed by the power of the living God, Creator of heaven and earth!

> You are next to be set free from addictions!
> You are next to see your entire family saved!
> You are next to reap an unprecedented harvest!
> You are next to awake and participate in changing our great nation!
> You are next to witness a fresh outpouring of the Holy Spirit!
> You are next for the breakthrough!
> You are next for the overflow!
> You are next for the healing!

Live like you are next, praise like you are next, dance like you are next, rejoice like you are next, worship like you are next, make a joyful noise like you are next, and stand up and walk like you are next.

Do you want to get well?

You. Are. Next!

Chapter Four

YOU ARE NEXT...

AS GOD CONFRONTS YOUR PRESENT

You are not defined by the likes of many;
you are defined by the love of One.

I WILL NEVER FORGET how I first glimpsed the presence of Jesus in my life. I did not experience a dramatic healing like the man at Bethesda or a voice booming down from heaven. But it shook me up and left me unsettled just the same.

Now, I will admit that if you saw me back in high school, you would probably say that it did not take much to shake me up! Most people would have called me a nerd, a good student interested in learning and determined to excel, who was fairly introverted and reserved. I hate to admit it, but I probably felt more excited about listening to Bon Jovi, Guns N' Roses, and Van Halen than hearing our pastor's sermons on Sunday. I preferred playing video games to studying the Bible and enjoyed watching MTV and old *Star Trek* reruns more than going to Sunday school. In other words, I looked and acted like a typical teenager in the 1980s!

After high school I wanted to attend college and study computers, becoming an engineer or some kind of programmer in the growing field of technology. I never imagined becoming a pastor. Only in my worst nightmares would I see myself standing in a pulpit preaching before thousands of people. Never in my wildest dreams could I imagine talking to the president of the United States, let alone offering to pray at his inauguration before a worldwide audience of millions of people.

But all that changed one night at age sixteen.

Most of the day had been like any other school day. I went to classes, came home, did homework, ate dinner with my family, and then prepared to watch TV for a few minutes before bed. Flipping channels, I clicked past familiar sitcoms with laugh tracks and melodramatic prime-time soap operas with wealthy oil tycoons wooing glamorous women. Then for some strange reason, I paused when I came to a well-known televangelist preaching before a crowd of people in a large auditorium. At the time, I had never really thought about him or his style of preaching much at all.

In that moment, however, as I sat before the screen of our big console color television set, I immediately received a message in my heart. "One day, Samuel, you will preach in front of people just like that! So many people!" I did not doubt it for a second, even though I had no idea at the time where it came from. In fact, it would have creeped me out if I had not felt the greatest sense of peace about it.

After the sermon ended, I sat there dazed and began flipping channels again. Had I imagined that message I heard inside my head? Maybe I just needed to go to bed already! I paused on the public television channel, airing a special on the life of Dr. Martin Luther King Jr. I knew of him, of course, as the iconic leader of the civil rights movement largely responsible for overturning segregation in our country. But when this program showed a clip of Dr. King preaching, something stirred inside me once again. "You will be doing that someday," this voice said. "You will preach and lead other people and tell them about God's love. You will be up there someday!"

I had no sense of needing to do anything differently, but I knew deep down that God has just given me a glimpse of His future for me. The next day and the weeks that followed, I could not shake the feeling of something significant having occurred that night as I sat in front of the TV in our family room. No one in our family had ever been in full-time ministry. My loving Christian parents created a warm, safe home for us, but I felt confident they had no aspirations for me as any kind of pastor or minister.

But after graduation my life began to take a different direction than any of us expected. The shy computer geek began to be transformed into a passionate young preacher on fire for God and the power of the gospel to change people's lives. Others began to notice, and one door after another opened for me to lead and to speak—at my church, at other churches within our denomination, and at conferences and community events. These opportunities opened before me so easily, so inevitably, that I knew without a doubt God had divinely appointed them. As more and more people and other pastors noticed me and extended invitations for me to preach, I felt as if I knew a secret. God had revealed this path to me all those years before, and now He started to unveil His big plan for my life.

FROM LAW TO LOVE

Compare my experience to that of the man beside the pool at Bethesda. His miracle, according to his observations and understanding, resided in waters moving there within the pool at Bethesda, with its five porches near the Sheep Gate corner of the temple courtyard in Jerusalem. But we find a problem with his perspective and resulting expectations: his breakthrough resided in a system established in the past.

Then Jesus came along. He easily could have said, "I will prompt the waters to move, and I will carry you in Myself." But He did not. Why? Because Jesus did not need to abide by this old system—He fulfilled it and thereby created a new system where all of us can experience God and His healing power in our lives.

Originally a system created by God prompted occasional supernatural intervention. This method of divine interaction permitted sinful human beings to experience relationship with the Holy One, the living God, the Almighty, Creator of heaven and earth. In general terms we have come to call this way of relating to God "the Law" because of its reliance on obeying commandments; maintaining strict habits of speech, thought, and behavior; and offering sacrifices, often a lamb or other animal, to atone for one's sins on a consistent, regular basis. We see the Law in effect throughout the Old Testament as the people of Israel struggle to love and serve God based on their own efforts.

Then God sent His only Son, Jesus Christ, to earth in the form of a man in order to radically change the way people related to God. Christ Himself became the system that guaranteed continual supernatural engagement. Perfect and sinless, Jesus took on all the sins of the world and became the unblemished Lamb of God, offered as an eternal sacrifice of atonement. "He himself is the sacrifice that atones for our sins—and not only our sins but the sins of all the world" (1 John 2:2, NLT). God replaced His Law with His love.

But people could not easily accept this change.

The Jewish people had been waiting for hundreds of years throughout many generations for God to send the Messiah, whom He promised to them by way of His prophets. As they watched their nation surrender to the Roman army and become another part of its vast global empire, the people of Israel became more desperate for God to deliver them—just as He had done before when they had been enslaved in Egypt. They expected the Messiah to raise an army and establish a kingdom that would restore Israel to its former glory.

Jesus turned those expectations upside down!

People waited for an event.

Jesus showed up and said, "I am the event!"

When Jesus shows up in your life, His presence always makes it the event!

CLOSE ENCOUNTERS

When you experience such an event and encounter Jesus, nothing stays the same. Sometimes your relationship with Him develops slowly and gradually blossoms into more. Looking back at my life now, I can see many little seeds God planted in my life to bring me to Him and to my purpose for His kingdom.

Other times, though, I know He often shows up unexpectedly and—*bam*!—nothing remains the same. Like the man at the pool of Bethesda experienced that day when he encountered Jesus, everything can change in the blink of an eye. Curiously enough, in those situations you might suddenly see the world around you quite differently than you did only seconds ago. Or, in the case of the apostle Paul, you might not see at all!

When we consider what it means for God to confront you in the midst of your situation right now in this present moment, we cannot find a more dramatic example than the showdown Paul, then known as Saul, had with the living Christ on the road to Damascus one day.

Meanwhile, Saul was still breathing out murderous threats against the Lord's disciples. He went to the high priest and asked him for letters to the synagogues in Damascus, so that if he found any there who belonged to the Way, whether men or women, he might take them as prisoners to Jerusalem. As he neared Damascus on his journey, suddenly a light from heaven flashed around him. He fell to the ground and heard a voice say to him, "Saul, Saul, why do you persecute me?"

"Who are you, Lord?" Saul asked.

"I am Jesus, whom you are persecuting," he replied. "Now get up and go into the city, and you will be told what you must do."

The men traveling with Saul stood there speechless; they heard the sound but did not see anyone. Saul got up from the ground, but when he opened his eyes he could see nothing. So they led him by the hand into Damascus. For three days he was blind, and did not eat or drink anything.

—ACTS 9:1–9

Talk about a close encounter of the best kind! Talk about changing the entire direction of your life! Just imagine Darth Vader traveling along looking for rebel Jedi warriors when suddenly he drops his lightsaber and collapses—because Saul had been that kind of guy! Only bad guys issue murderous threats like some fire-breathing dragon on the loose. In some ways, any fantasy creature pales in comparison to Paul because he believed in doing things precisely by the letter of the Law.

You see, Saul had been raised in a strict Jewish religious household and taught to believe no one could be righteous without strictly adhering to God's Law. Jewish people who took this Law seriously and lived righteously had favor with God, but only as long as they obeyed every last detail of the Law. This included not only following the Ten Commandments—as we call the ten edicts God gave to Moses for the people of Israel—but also the strict dietary, social, and cultural laws recorded in Deuteronomy and Leviticus. Saul must have heard about Jesus' claims that He fulfilled the Law and set all people free by God's grace.

But Saul did not buy it—not for a minute!

So not only did he go out hunting followers of Jesus with their grace-based lifestyle known as the Way, but Saul also made sure his prisoners would have no legal or religious recourse after he captured them. He had the high priest in Jerusalem write letters to the priests in charge of other synagogues in nearby cities authorizing Saul to arrest any of these believers in their communities.

Notice too that the text specifies both men and women could be taken as prisoners. Usually only men would be charged, arrested, and taken into custody in this ancient culture that considered women to be personal property, not public criminals. But not so in this case. Any woman participating in this new cult forming around the carpenter from Nazareth would be captured and considered just as culpable as a man. Saul intended to eradicate this errant system of false beliefs and its adherents before it grew and went any further.

But then he met Jesus.

A bright light flashed in the sky as Saul fell to the ground. Then a voice boomed out, "Why are you doing this? Why are you persecuting Me?"

Saul, like most of us, asked for the identity of his apparent assailant. "Who are You?" he cried.

"I am Jesus, the One whom you are persecuting. Get up, go to the city, and you will find out what to do next."

While we might be tempted to think Saul had little choice, he, like all of us, got to choose how to respond to such an unexpected encounter. He could easily have become angry and upset, more determined than ever to seek out the Jesus groupies who must surely be responsible for his attack. But that theory would not have held water because the event left the men traveling with Saul speechless. They knew they had not engaged in any kind of human confrontation. They had not been ambushed by bandits or hijacked by foreigners. They had experienced a divine encounter with the living God!

STRAIGHT STREET

When you have an encounter with Jesus, others might struggle to accept your transformation. They might be more familiar or even more comfortable with the person you have been. This certainly happened to a dangerous bounty hunter like Saul, a well-known persecutor of believers. In fact, Saul-turned-Paul would face this problem with his reputation frequently.

Later, after he had been saved by grace and filled with the Holy Spirit, Paul often explained his life prior to Christ: "I am a Jew, born in Tarsus of Cilicia, but brought up in this city. I studied under Gamaliel and was thoroughly trained in the law of our ancestors. I was just as zealous for God as any of you are today. I persecuted the followers of this Way to their death, arresting both men and women and throwing them into prison, as the high priest and all the Council can themselves testify" (Acts 22:3–5). Paul even admitted that not only had he gone from one synagogue to another to beat and imprison Jesus' followers, but he had tacitly given his approval while an angry mob martyred Stephen for his Christian faith, choosing to guard the coats of those stoning an innocent preacher of the gospel (v. 20).

Not surprisingly, other believers struggled to accept Saul's encounter as authentic. A follower of the Way named Ananias resisted the Lord's prompting to go and tend to Saul, but then God made it explicitly clear that he had big plans for this man who had once persecuted believers. As we see, Saul was indeed never the same man again following his encounter on the road.

> In Damascus there was a disciple named Ananias. The Lord called to him in a vision, "Ananias!"
>
> "Yes, Lord," he answered.
>
> The Lord told him, "Go to the house of Judas on Straight Street and ask for a man from Tarsus named Saul, for he is praying. In a vision he has seen a man named Ananias come and place his hands on him to restore his sight."
>
> "Lord," Ananias answered, "I have heard many reports about this man and all the harm he has done to your holy people in Jerusalem. And he has come here with authority from the chief priests to arrest all who call on your name."
>
> But the Lord said to Ananias, "Go! This man is my chosen instrument to proclaim my name to the Gentiles and their kings and to the people of Israel. I will show him how much he must suffer for my name."
>
> Then Ananias went to the house and entered it. Placing his hands on Saul, he said, "Brother Saul, the Lord—Jesus,

who appeared to you on the road as you were coming here—has sent me so that you may see again and be filled with the Holy Spirit." Immediately, something like scales fell from Saul's eyes, and he could see again. He got up and was baptized, and after taking some food, he regained his strength.

—Acts 9:10–19

When we wander down our own Straight Street, we often have to face up to old habits and patterns of living. Sometimes we may have to surrender our addictions and sinful behavior at the foot of the cross daily or even hourly. Sometimes God removes them from our lives like the scales falling from Saul's eyes. Suddenly we too see clearly that our old lives are over, and we sense God calling us to something new. Others may struggle with accepting our new lives, but if they know the source of our transformation—the grace of God through the power of Jesus Christ and the indwelling of His Holy Spirit— then they know how immediately God can work.

Sometimes after God confronts you in your present, you may struggle to get back on your feet again. I find it significant that Saul required assistance from others for his healing to be complete. First, he had to be led into the city because he could not see, and then he needed Ananias' help. Ananias called Saul, "Brother," laid hands on him, and prayed over him as the scales of blindness fell away and the Spirit of God filled his heart.

> Whoever you used to be, whatever you have done, wherever you have been—these things no longer matter when you meet Jesus.

The impact happened immediately! Saul got up, and what did he do? Even before he ate some food, he got baptized! The man had not eaten for at least three days, and yet once he encountered Jesus, Saul hungered for God more than for food. After his conversion Saul became a new creature in Christ known as Paul.

Whoever you used to be, whatever you have done, wherever you have been—these things no longer matter when you meet Jesus. He wipes the slate clean. He heals your paralysis. He breaks your generational curses. He empowers you to do what you could not do before. He gives you a new life through the power of His Spirit in you!

STORMS, SHIPWRECKS, AND SNAKES

Saul fulfilled the calling God placed on his life with flying colors. When God told Ananias, "This man is my chosen instrument to proclaim my name to the Gentiles and their kings and to the people of Israel," He meant it!

> Saul spent several days with the disciples in Damascus. At once he began to preach in the synagogues that Jesus is the Son of God. All those who heard him were

astonished and asked, "Is not he the man who raised havoc in Jerusalem among those who call on this name? And hasn't he come here to take them as prisoners to the chief priests?" Yet Saul grew more and more powerful and baffled the Jews living in Damascus by proving that Jesus is the Messiah.

After many days had gone by, there was a conspiracy among the Jews to kill him, but Saul learned of their plan. Day and night they kept close watch on the city gates in order to kill him. But his followers took him by night and lowered him in a basket through an opening in the wall.

When he came to Jerusalem, he tried to join the disciples, but they were all afraid of him, not believing that he really was a disciple. But Barnabas took him and brought him to the apostles. He told them how Saul on his journey had seen the Lord and that the Lord had spoken to him, and how in Damascus he had preached fearlessly in the name of Jesus. So Saul stayed with them and moved about freely in Jerusalem, speaking boldly in the name of the Lord.

—ACTS 9:19–28

Notice that after his personal encounter with Jesus, Saul began doing the very thing he had once violently opposed—sharing the good news of grace through Jesus Christ. Not only did he get baptized right away, but Saul also began preaching shortly after his conversion. When God confronts you in your present, you will suddenly start moving out of your comfort zone and into your grace zone. You will take risks that you would never have taken before. You will accomplish things that you would never have considered attempting before. You will no longer worry what others think about you and what you do.

I learned this firsthand, my friend. That shy, reserved, tech-loving Trekkie who planned on a quiet life as a computer engineer became this fired-up, pulpit-pounding, God-praising, Spirit-guided preacher, teacher, and leader. If I had not responded to my encounters with God, I would have missed out on many blessings. It has not always been easy, but I would not trade the adventure of faith God continues to guide me on for anything in this world.

As Saul found out, though, living out our faith has never been about taking the easy road. Right away Saul began getting grief for the dramatic way he preached and evangelized. And he must have been a powerful megaphone for God because some of the Jews wanted him dead! I cannot help but wonder if some of Saul's former colleagues and associates turned on him, furious that they had lost their top lieutenant in the pursuit and persecution of believers. Surely they considered Saul a traitor!

Saul's new family in Christ, however, clearly had his back. Knowing these Jews monitored the city gates day and night, a group of Christians hid their new brother Saul in a basket and lowered him like a bushel of wheat to the other side. Yes, some believers still feared him and wondered if Saul's behavior was some kind of ruse, but others, such as Barnabas, trusted God's guidance in accepting and helping Saul.

From there Saul began traveling, first with Barnabas and then later with Timothy and other believers, teaching and preaching to Gentiles in foreign lands. Somewhere along the way Saul began using the Greek version of his name, Paul, which is how he became best known. I suspect the change not only helped him escape his bad reputation as a bounty hunter but also reflected the new identity he found in Christ. Paul went on to endure beatings, arrests, shipwrecks, and snakebites. In fact, I wrote an entire book about Paul's unbelievable journey from Jerusalem to Rome: *Shake Free: How to Deal With the Storms, Shipwrecks, and Snakes in Your Life.*[1]

While making his many journeys, Paul frequently wrote letters, or epistles as they were called, to the communities of believers in the distant ports he had visited. Many of these letters divinely inspired by the Holy Spirit became part of the New Testament in the Bible. His words continue to speak to us as God's Word today, and his example reminds us that when God confronts your present, you need to surrender to His love.

Paul faithfully served the Lord and proclaimed the gospel message for the rest of his life. He never forgot though that God's grace and God's grace alone was the source of his identity, his authority, and his reality. In a letter to the church at Corinth, Paul wrote, "For I am the least of the apostles and do not even deserve to be called an apostle, because I persecuted the church of God. But by the grace of God I am what I am, and his grace to me was not without effect. No, I worked harder than all of them—yet not I, but the grace of God that was with me" (1 Cor. 15:9–10).

GOD AT WORK IN YOU

An authentic encounter with the grace of God continues to change people today. Just as we see with the man at Bethesda and the conversion of Saul, the presence and power of Jesus changes everything. When Christ confronts your present, He conveys a new message about your identity and purpose. I believe Jesus says:

> I am not here to change the things around you—I am here to change the things *inside* you!

> I am not here simply to change your circumstances—I am here to change *you* in the midst of your circumstances!

> I have not come to stir up the waters in front of you—I have come to stir up the *faith inside* you!

But too often we continue to ponder our paralysis and wallow by the waters. You see, paralysis doesn't only happen to your body. When you refuse to experience the fullness of God's Spirit through the presence of Jesus in your life, paralysis strikes your thinking. Your faith freezes. You disable your strength, hope, and power.

However, God does not confront you right here and right now about your power—but about His power! We can get so full of ourselves and our problems sometimes. In the love of one Christian brother for his sisters and brothers in the family of Christ, let me tell you something: get over yourself! I know that might sound harsh, but as severe as that sounded, it would be far worse to miss out on what God has for you! Do not let the devil keep your eyes only on your paralysis and what you cannot do. Do not buy his lies that you are not good enough or strong enough or powerful enough.

It does not depend on you—if it did, you would remain paralyzed!

> In the love of one Christian brother for his sisters and brothers in the family of Christ, let me tell you something: get over yourself!

The Word promises us that "it is God who works in you to will and to act in order to fulfill his good purpose" (Phil. 2:13). Stop crawling on your belly when you can stand on your feet and step out in faith! Quit writhing on the ground when you can hold your head up high and lift your hands toward heaven, praising God for all He has done and will continue to do for you!

Do not look at your ability—look at His anointing.

Do not rely on your potential—rely on His power.

Do not focus on who you are in Him—focus on who He is in you!

Stop asking what you can do through Him—ask what He can do through you.

My friend, you and I are not blessed because of *where* we are; we are blessed because of *whose* we are! God wants to work in your life, to lift you up and make you well.

Will you let Him? Will you obey and stand up? Will you let go of the ground and grasp the hand of your Savior? If you want to experience the healing transformation that results when you embrace God's presence in your life, then tell Him! Pray to God right now and let Him know you feel ready to walk. You have grown tired of waiting and wondering, watching and worrying. You will no longer wait on someone else to lift you up and take you to the waters. From now on you refuse to live under the old systems that keep you paralyzed.

Instead you drink the living water of Jesus.

You let go of who you once were.

You prepare for your turn, right here and right now in the present!

You are next!

Chapter Five

YOU ARE NEXT...

AS GOD RELEASES YOU FROM YOUR PAST

God is not interested in renovating
your past. He stands committed
to releasing your future.

SAMUEL. SAMMY. PASTOR Sam. Sam I Am. Sambo. Pichi. Rico.

Throughout my life, I have been called a number of names—variations of my given name, terms of endearment bestowed by friends and family, and even a few resulting from mispronunciation, misunderstanding, or misadventure.

My buddies in high school usually called me Sammy or Rico (after a character in the 1980s *Miami Vice* television series). My mother and father always preferred using my nickname—Pichi—especially when wanting to underline the seriousness of their communication. "Pichi, have you finished your homework?" my mom would ask. Or whenever my dad said, "Pichi, we need to talk," I knew I must have done something wrong.

As an adult I have left most of the silly nicknames behind. My wife and close friends usually call me just Sam, while much of the time these days I am called Pastor Sam due to my vocation. Of course, when someone calls or emails and addresses me as Mr. Rodriguez, I am almost always correct in identifying them as someone who does not know me.

In addition to derivatives of my name I have been called a lot worse too—put-downs and insults having nothing to do with my identity but everything to do with the biased perceptions and personal prejudices of others. Some people even today try to drag me into the past by using certain names to bully, intimidate, and disparage who I am and what I am about. But my name, Samuel, means God has heard, and so I cling to my identity in Christ, knowing that I am not tied to what anyone else calls me.

I offer you this same truth, my friend.

STUCK IN THE PAST

No matter your name, what you have done, where you live, or the kind of paralysis you may have overcome in your life, other people will try to tie you to your past mistakes, to identify you by your faults, and to label you based on their limited grasp of your true self. They may even temporarily convince you that you can never escape your past and start over in the freedom of the present. Even when they see you walking in front of them, no longer paralyzed by your past, they may still treat you like an invalid, a victim and not a victor.

Some might label you with names that reflect who you once were rather than who God has redeemed you to become. Others might think of you as a liar, a cheater, a gossip, an adulterer, an addict, or a thief. Even when they attempt to make the names and labels more socially acceptable, like workaholic or perfectionist, these monikers remain tied to your past and not your future, and consequently keep you paralyzed in the present.

While society, friends, or strangers may identify you by past issues, God views you in the fullness of your new relationship with Him through His Son, Jesus Christ. Even when you label yourself based on your past feelings, habits, and behaviors, those labels can inhibit your ability to walk by faith. When God looks at you, He sees beyond any names, labels, issues, and struggles of your past.

In fact, He has promised to give you a new name, a secret name known only by you and God, a name that reflects your freedom in Christ. The Bible says, "Whoever has ears, let them hear what the Spirit says to the churches. To the one who is victorious, I will give some of the hidden manna. I will also give that person a white stone with a new name written on it, known only to the one who receives it" (Rev. 2:17).

While Bible scholars debate the exact meaning of this promise, most seem to agree on the symbolism of the white stone. Apparently in ancient times when they brought someone to trial, the jury delivered their verdict in the form of a black stone for guilty and a white stone for not guilty. Having God give you a new name written on a white stone reflects the way your sins have been forgiven. Christ's sacrifice on the cross erases your guilt and frees you from the penalty of death. You can now live an earthly life of blessing and abundance and look forward to eternal life with God in heaven. When God looks at you, He sees beyond your past issues and present struggles and focuses on your faith-fueled future.

Sadly, though, many people seem unable to let go of the labels that others have stuck on them. Maybe some do not let go because they grew comfortable with their labels. Even if they know this is not who they are, they would rather accept the role written for them by other people than go off script and be the unique individual God made them to be. Some dwell on past mistakes while others cling to past milestones, living in the glory days of their youth as the star athlete, the pretty cheerleader, the academic achiever, or the most popular.

When I have returned to Pennsylvania and run into former classmates, I am always amazed that some of them have never traveled outside the state. They still try to be the person they used to be—the class clown, the prodigy, the beauty queen, or the bad boy or bad girl. Instead of maturing and growing beyond adolescence, a few individuals seem stuck there, working hard to look the same, sound the same, and be the same.

But clinging to the past inhibits true maturity. It hinders your progress and prevents growth. Like an adult trying to wear the clothes of a child, it no longer fits who you have become.

I am not saying you have to leave your hometown to break free from your past, but sometimes seeing yourself in new environments and stepping outside the roles and labels others use to limit you can work wonders. Yes, it can be incredibly tempting to stay in one spot and think, "I am OK here. I have always known this, so at least it feels familiar. I know everybody, and they know me. I am too scared to risk leaving all that I know to start over, meet new people, or change careers. There might be more for me if I dared to follow God to where He wants to take me. But there might not be. No, I will just stay put."

> Clinging to the past inhibits true maturity. It hinders your progress and prevents growth.

Some people know they do not want to keep living in the past, but they feel stuck. They seem unsure how to break free, and they wonder if they even can ever truly leave their past behind. They worry about not fitting in if they move forward, about not having any label at all, or about losing what they already have. They sense God calling them to follow Him into a new future, but anytime their faith gets stretched, they allow their fears to snap them back to the past like some kind of invisible rubber band.

If you find yourself in this group, it means you struggle to trust that God goes with you, His Holy Spirit lives within you, and He will make a way for you. Jesus would never have told the man beside the pool of Bethesda to get up and walk if He did not have the supernatural power to make it happen instantaneously. But you have to trust, to choose to at least try to get on your feet and stand up, even if you cannot feel your legs and you fear falling to the ground yet again.

Jesus did not carry this man. Christ did not hold him up and gently lead him around until the feeling came back into his paralyzed legs. The Lord did not hand this man a cane and tell him it would take a few months of physical therapy.

No, Jesus said, "Take up your mat and walk!"

But God cannot pry us loose from our past if we will not stand.

Do you want to get well?

Then you must be willing to leave the past behind.

NO LAUGHING MATTER

When we refuse to let go of our past, we seal our own destruction. Jesus wants to heal us, but instead we keep our eyes on the ground and continue laying down instead of standing up to walk into the new future He has for us. Perhaps we find the best illustration of this tragic choice in the Old Testament when God chose to destroy two cities, Sodom and Gomorrah, where evil ran rampant. These two empires of immorality had become quicksand pits of greed, filth, perversity, and every kind of sin imaginable.

> **When we refuse to let go of our past, we seal our own destruction.**

Finally God had enough. But before He destroyed these twin cities of terror, the Lord recognized the few faithful people living there, namely Lot and his family, and sent angels to warn them. God gave them only one simple condition to avoid being consumed by imminent fiery destruction, and one woman chose to ignore this condition.

So Lot went out and spoke to his sons-in-law, who were pledged to marry his daughters. He said, "Hurry and get out of this place, because the LORD is about to destroy the city!" But his sons-in-law thought he was joking.

With the coming of dawn, the angels urged Lot, saying, "Hurry! Take your wife and your two daughters who are here, or you will be swept away when the city is punished."

When he hesitated, the men grasped his hand and the hands of his wife and of his two daughters and led them safely out of the city, for the LORD was merciful to them. As soon as they had brought them out, one of them said, "Flee for your lives! Don't look back, and don't stop anywhere in the plain! Flee to the mountains or you will be swept away!"

…Then the LORD rained down burning sulfur on Sodom and Gomorrah—from the LORD out of the heavens. Thus he overthrew those cities and the entire plain, destroying all those living in the cities—and also the vegetation in the land. But Lot's wife looked back, and she became a pillar of salt.

—Genesis 19:14–17, 24–26

We do not know this woman's name; the Bible simply identifies her as the wife of Lot, the nephew of Abraham. Perhaps we do not know her name because she could not let go of her past and, therefore, she never discovered her identity within the future God wanted to give her. Even before she appears in this scene, I find it striking that Lot's sons-in-law not only refused to heed his warning—a warning directly from God's angels—but they thought Lot was joking. Some people refuse to listen to God's messages or to accept His invitations.

Can you imagine if the man at Bethesda had laughed when Jesus told him to get up and walk? What if he had told the Lord, "You must be joking! Do You not know I am paralyzed?"

While we may not laugh at God or assume that He is joking, we sometimes allow our doubts and disbeliefs to have the same impact. Because we cannot come up with a rational, logical grasp of the miracle God wants to do for us, we dismiss the opportunity and remain fixed on the past. We assume the past provides us with probabilities and known expectations, an understanding of what we can anticipate to come. But God wants to break us free from the past by continually inviting us to stand up and walk into His glorious future.

When God wants to release you from your past, do not consider it a laughing matter.

NO TURNING BACK

Another compelling detail in this story emerges in the repeated expression of God's mercy and compassion. His angels did not just deliver their message and head back to heaven. No, they stuck around to do everything they could to make sure this family escaped from the fiery destruction raining down around them. Before the passage above, two angels visited Lot at home and delivered their first warning (Gen. 19:12–13).

In fact, the men of Sodom—and the Scripture says *all* men, both young and old—were so depraved that they surrounded Lot's house and demanded sex with his two guests (vv. 4–5). Horrified, Lot begged his neighbors and city residents not to violate the safety and hospitality his guests deserved. Lot even went so far as to offer his own virgin daughters to satisfy the mob's lusts. Just as the angry throng threatened Lot, the angels pulled him back inside and blinded all the men outside so they could not find their way into the house.

I do not know about you, but if I found myself in such a situation, I would take God's warning very seriously. I would waste no time getting out of there as quickly as possible! But Lot took the time to warn his other family members, which the angels graciously prompted him to do, before dawn. But as the sun's first light sliced into the horizon that morning, the angels insisted that Lot, his wife, and their two daughters flee without delay.

Curiously enough, their warning must not have registered with Lot because verse 16 says that "when he hesitated," the angels grabbed his hands and the hands of his family members and led them "safely out of the city." Maybe the uncertainty of where they would go and how they would get there paralyzed them. Despite all they had seen and experienced, maybe somehow they still resisted leaving their home, the place where they dwelled. As bad as it was, perhaps they preferred the safety of the past over the faith required to find their future.

Before we judge them or wonder how they could think this, we might consider our own moments of hesitation. I heard an old saying: "Better the devil you know than the devil you do not." In other words, sometimes the terrible conditions you already face seem more manageable than the unknown fears and anxious anguish lurking ahead.

For this reason many people in abusive relationships keep taking the abuse rather than risk leaving and facing life alone. Other people trapped in addictions continue suffering the consequences of their physical deterioration rather than risk getting help and facing the painful roots of their addiction. Still others stay in dead-end jobs and terrible neighborhoods. We cling to the past because fear of the future overwhelms us.

God consistently pursues us, though. He refuses to leave us within the prisons of our past when Jesus has broken the bars and set all prisoners free. In the same way that the angels took Lot and his family by the hand, God extends His hand to us even today. He wants us to leave the past behind and follow Him up beyond the chaos of past mistakes, past struggles, and past pain. The climb will not be easy, but He will go with us. Jesus gives us the power and the strength needed to walk by faith and leave past trauma behind us.

We only have to do our part. Just as the angels instructed Lot and his family, God only asks one simple thing: do not look back! Do not get stuck in the past. Do not turn your eyes on where you have been because when you do, you cannot see where God wants to take you.

You cannot turn back after God has turned your life around.

Have you ever tried to drive forward while looking only in the rearview mirror or at the video screen that comes on when you put your car in reverse? While it may not be impossible, two things happen as a result. First, you cannot go the normal speed, which causes considerable delay. Second, you will crash. If you do not watch the road in front of you while driving, then sooner or later you will hit another vehicle, a pedestrian, a telephone pole, a concrete barrier, or even a building.

Living your life in the past amounts to the same thing. Someone once said that the definition of *insanity* is making the same mistake over and over again while expecting a different result. When you live in the past, you get stuck in a groove, like an old LP record player with a needle stuck, going around and around on the scratched vinyl.

My friend, you do not have to live this way!

Jesus came to heal your paralysis of the past.

But you have to stand up.

You have to take God's hand…

…before the past destroys you.

THE LONGER YOU LINGER

Theologians, scholars, archaeologists, and Bible readers have debated for centuries the reason Lot's wife looked back. No one actually knows, however, because she turned into a block of salt before anyone could ask her.

I believe she just could not let go of her past. Sodom contained her home and all she knew. As terrible, wicked, and depraved as we find it, she did not have to worry about being surprised there by unfamiliar faces and unexpected events. So in direct violation of God's command not to look back, Lot's wife turned her head and lost her humanity. As a result, instead of knowing her by her name, we know her story as a cautionary tale so important that Jesus Himself later referenced it.

> It was the same in the days of Lot. People were eating and drinking, buying and selling, planting and building. But the day Lot left Sodom, fire and sulfur rained down from heaven and destroyed them all.
> It will be just like this on the day the Son of Man is revealed. On that day no one who is on the housetop, with possessions inside, should go down to get them. Likewise, no one in the field should go back for anything. Remember Lot's wife! Whoever tries to keep their life will lose it, and whoever loses their life will preserve it.
> —LUKE 17:28–33

Lot's wife became a pillar to her past instead of finding the fortress of God's future. Jesus told us we have no time to go back and recover items in the face of an imminent divine encounter with the living God. Like going back inside a burning house to save clothes, furniture, or jewelry, you risk your life by retreating into reverse. If you flew on a plane that made an emergency landing on the water, you would not be worried about your carry-on luggage, purse, or laptop! You would be focused on preserving your life in the face of such immediate danger.

Nonetheless, we all have moments when, like Lot and his family, we hesitate when we know God calls us to move on from the past. What person or thing in your life tempts you to pause in the midst of God's invitation to move forward? It might be your insecurity preventing you from applying for that job you know God wants you to have. It might be your unwillingness to start a family with your spouse even though you know the Lord has revealed the time has come. Maybe you have heard God's call to start a new ministry or volunteer in your community, but you continue to stay "too busy." Perhaps you need to confront an addiction in your own life or that of someone you love, but past failures impede your initiative.

It can be hard to shake the past when you hesitate.

The longer you linger, the harder it gets.

The longer you delay, the more you risk your future.

Lot's wife reminds us to follow God's guidance to our future instead of looking over our shoulder at our past. God directs us to focus our eyes on Him, trusting that He will guide our steps as we climb the mountain above the valley of our victimhood. Lot's wife could not stop clinging to where she had been, which resulted in her complete devastation.

> **God does not want to erase your past, but He does want to transform it.**

It reminds me of the way I recycle boxes to mail packages to our kids. I will grab an empty box from the garage, pack whatever we plan to send, and seal it up. But then comes the most important part: I have to place a new address on the old box—otherwise it will go to its past destination, not where I now want it to go now!

You have been released from your past by the power of the blood of Jesus Christ.

You have been redirected to your new eternal destination.

You have been redeemed for the fulfillment of the joy set before you.

God does not want to erase your past, but He does want to transform it. In His Word, God tells us, "See, I am doing a new thing! Now it springs up; do you not perceive it? I am making a way in the wilderness and streams in the wasteland" (Isa. 43:19). My friend, you need to see your past as a barren, desolate place of ashes and salt blocks. But if you allow God to heal your paralysis, that wasteland can start to bloom and flourish with blessing!

MOVING UP THE MOUNTAIN

When I visited Israel, I heard about a centuries-old salt formation near the Dead Sea at Mount Sodom. While no one knows if this natural edifice started out as Lot's wife, it certainly serves as a reminder of her fate. I find it incredibly sad to know that instead of a shrine commemorating her obedience and faithfulness, only a dry, dusty rock formation of sodium chloride remains. Instead of moving up the mountain, Lot's wife became a monument to lost momentum.

Consider how differently her story might have ended. For example, we see a similar kind of stubborn resistance to God's leading in the case of Jonah. Instructed by God to go to the city of Nineveh and warn its residents of their imminent destruction unless they repented, Jonah ran away. He tried to go the opposite direction and escape the place where God needed him to serve—and consequently ended up in the belly of a fish! But Jonah eventually repented and allowed God to use him to go to Nineveh and do what God needed him to do. Jonah surrendered his shackles to the past in order to fulfill the purpose for which God made him.

Similarly, we see the way many of those included in the faith hall of fame in Hebrews chapter 11 made the same choice to leave their past behind. Instead of looking back in destruction, they chose to walk by faith. Scripture says, "Faith shows the reality of what we hope for; it is the evidence of things we cannot see" (Heb. 11:1, NLT). And the pioneers of faith included here moved beyond the paralysis of their past to procure the promise of God's power. Noah, Abraham, Sarah, Isaac, Jacob, Joseph, Moses, and on and on—each individual chose to move forward instead of backward.

If you want to experience the fullness of God's healing in the midst of those paralyzed areas of your life, you must follow the Lord. You must heed His voice and obey His commands. You must leave the place you used to live behind you. You must be willing to travel light and follow the sound of God's voice.

And leaving your old life for the place God wants to take you involves so much more than geography. While He very well might want you to move across town, out of state, or to the other side of the world, God often wants to see movement in your heart. He wants you to stop carrying around baggage from the past that serves no purpose in your present and only slows you down in reaching your future.

Can you relate? How much baggage do you carry with you from the past on a daily basis? Maybe you have accumulated it from the arguments, conflicts, and grudges in your marriage, from the painful disappointments you have experienced when your spouse has let you down. But what if you could forgive your spouse the way God forgives you? What if you let go of your past expectations and old grudges so that the Lord can lead you into new heights of forgiveness, love, and grace?

Maybe you have been settling for less than you know God has for you in your career. You watch others finish their degrees, get promoted, and enjoy doing what God made them to do, but you do nothing about moving your own dreams forward. What if you let go of old excuses and past limitations? What if you followed God's call to step out and begin doing what He created you to do?

> What if you let go of your past expectations and old grudges so that the Lord can lead you into new heights of forgiveness, love, and grace?

Maybe you want to be a better parent to your kids, but you will not forgive yourself for past failures. Perhaps you need to ask forgiveness from friends you have wounded with your words so that He can take your relationships to a deeper, God-honoring place. Or maybe you need new friends, ones who will hold your hand as the angels did with Lot and guide you toward the Lord, instead of old friends, or people claiming to be your friends, who keep you trapped in the past.

We all have areas of our lives where we find safety by dwelling in the past. We may have invited God into most areas of our lives but not all areas. And in those secret areas we remain a prisoner to the past, unable to move forward and increasingly unwilling to try.

Am I talking to you? Does your abuse keep you paralyzed by the fear that you might feel that powerless again? Does your addiction, even when in recovery, keep you paralyzed with fear that you will slip back into it? Does anxiety keep you stuck in place because, after everything you have been through, after everything you have lost—jobs, relationships, homes, and money—you wonder when the next crisis will happen or the next catastrophe will crash down on you? Does your status, that veneer of success, accomplishment, and material success you have worked for all your life, keep you tied up in knots as you strive to stay afloat?

Whatever happened in your past, surrender it at the foot of the cross.

It will be hard, but God never leaves you, and He will strengthen you. He will send His angels to guard you, and He will guide you out of destruction and into new life. There will be growing pains. You will struggle and stumble sometimes. You will grumble like the people of Israel did after God rescued them from slavery in Egypt, complaining that life seemed better back in the past compared with the discomfort of the present. Struggling to glimpse the Promised Land, they wanted to settle for less.

You alone must make the choice, my friend.

In many ways it seems very simple: forward or backward.

The man beside the pool of Bethesda had been paralyzed for thirty-eight years. Why should he ever expect to walk again? Why should he dare hope for a miracle? Why should he not look back and resign himself to remaining flat on the ground for the rest of his life?

Why? Because of Jesus Christ!

Jesus conquered your past and opened the door to your glorious future.

Jesus broke through your past and guides you beyond where you started.

Jesus overcame your past so that you might know complete healing.

I cannot urge you strongly enough: do whatever you need to do to break the chains of your past and all the labels still clinging to you. If you are serious about growing in your faith, then hesitate no longer. Stop looking back! Quit pretending to look ahead while your neck stiffens from staring behind you!

Take God's hand and let Him lead you beyond where you have been. Let Him take you to a summit you have never imagined in your wildest dreams. You can get there, but only if you trust Him.

As I write this, I feel led to declare some things over you before you turn the page to the next chapter. I believe God will release you from your past, and I invite you to join me in declaring these affirmations over yourself.

No longer will you remain flat on the ground of your past. You will choose to get on your feet.

You will choose to follow God forward, step by step, up
  the mountain.

Your past has no claim on you.

You belong to God.

You are a child of the King.

You are a new creation in Christ.

The time has come to step out of the paralysis of the past.

The time has come for you to stop letting others hold you
  back.

If you want to be released from your past, then remember
only one thing:

You are next!

Chapter Six

YOU ARE NEXT...

AS GOD SPEAKS INTO YOUR FUTURE

Stop saying, "Look what the devil
did" and start shouting, "Look
what the Lord has done!"

H

OW CAN YOU be in tomorrow when I am still in today?"

My five-year-old daughter's voice revealed both her excitement and disbelief when I made my first trip to Australia to preach at a conference. Eva stayed home with the children, and the difference in our time zones—a whopping nineteen hours—meant that my call to tell the kids good night at bedtime took place in the afternoon of the next day there in Sydney.

"Well," I said, "you remember how I showed you the way we can move the hands on the clock? And then we looked at the globe, and I showed you how the earth spins on its axis as it orbits around the sun?" At the time, back before I left, I thought she understood, but suddenly I felt unsure. In fact I felt unsure that I understood it anymore!

"I remember," she said. "But I don't see how you can be in the future and ahead of us here at home! Is it like *Star Wars* or something?"

"Not really," I said, trying to wind up the expensive international call. "I can explain it again once I get home, OK? Now brush your teeth and get in bed. Mommy will read your bedtime story, but I am going to pray with you right now."

I prayed for my daughter and the rest of our family, keeping my prayer similar to what I usually prayed in Sacramento to tuck her in. After our shared "Amen," I said, "I love you! And I will be home soon."

She paused and said, "I love you too, Daddy, but I just have one question before we hang up."

"What, honey?" I said.

"What will the weather be like tomorrow? Is it raining where you are? Because if it rains tomorrow, then I want to make sure I find my galoshes tonight!"

Even though my daughter is all grown up now, that precious story still makes me smile.

TOMORROW IS YESTERDAY

Time travel remains one of the basic conventions of science fiction stories. While I had not traveled through time, to my young daughter it certainly seemed as if I had. As I mentioned, I am a die-hard Trekkie and grew up watching the original *Star Trek* series in syndication as well as its spin-off *Star Trek: The Next Generation.* You do not have to be a fan to guess that traveling backward and forward in time—usually due to a black hole or some other anomaly in space—made up the plot of quite a few episodes.

In fact, one of the episodes in the first season of the original *Star Trek* series, entitled "Tomorrow Is Yesterday," involved the USS *Enterprise* going back to Earth in the 1960s, a clever wink to the time of the original broadcast. When an Air Force pilot spots the Enterprise and gets caught in its tractor beam, Captain Kirk saves the man, named John Christopher, by beaming him aboard. Unfortunately, Christopher quickly sees that Kirk, Spock, and the crew have traveled from the future and, much like my young daughter, tries to make sense of the situation.

Fearing the consequences to history if they let Christopher return to Earth with knowledge of the future, at first Kirk and Spock decide to take him with them back to their time, an unspecified stardate in the twenty-third century. Then Spock, perusing history, realizes that while Captain Christopher himself seemed to live an ordinary, unremarkable life, he would go on to father a son who would lead the first expedition to Saturn. Basically, removing one domino from history would set in motion a topple effect, changing everything! Kirk manages to wipe Christopher's memory and get him back to his time, as well as take the photos snapped of their ship, but the show raises several intriguing questions about the way our present decisions have a ripple effect into future consequences.

Coming back from the fictional future to the reality of the ancient world, consider the man at the pool of Bethesda once more. With the paralyzed man's encounter with Jesus as our basis, we have looked at the way God confronts our present moment and requires us to make a choice about whether or not we want to get well. And then we considered the new life we experience when God releases us from the past. But now we will explore the impact on your life when God speaks into your future!

> **When you encounter Jesus Christ, He draws a line between your past and your future; they will never be the same!**

If the man at Bethesda had been content to remain paralyzed, his future would have mirrored his past. He would have continued to be a victim of the debilitating physical limitations hindering his mobility. Day after day he would have remained a familiar figure there at Bethesda, watching others being healed upon entering the pool right after the angel stirred its waters—lying on the ground, crawling like a worm, and never fast enough to receive the healing splash.

When you encounter Jesus Christ, He draws a line between your past and your future; they will never be the same! When you accept His invitation to be healed and to stand up and walk by faith, you no longer know what your future, which once seemed so bleak and predictable, will be like. It will actually exceed anything you can imagine or make happen for yourself. But it all starts with your willingness to engage with the present, relinquish the past, and receive the future God has for you.

Your future matters to God, and what He has called you to do can be accomplished by no other. You do not need *Star Trek* or me to tell you because God's Word makes it clear that He wants to do amazing things in our lives if we will only let Him.

YOU TALKING TO ME?

As we have seen, the man at Bethesda was not the only underdog whose future transformed after crossing paths with the power of the living God. Time and time again in the pages of the Bible we see God choosing people the world overlooks, from a shepherd boy who became king to a ruthless mercenary who became the apostle to the Gentiles. One of my favorites just happens to reveal one of the most significant transformations.

Like geeky teenager Peter Parker becoming Spider-Man or scrawny Steve Rogers morphing into Captain America, Gideon started out as perhaps the most unlikely hero of the Jewish people. In fact, I think Gideon's story would be right at home on the big screen as a superhero epic with all the CGI green-screen special effects we can produce with today's technology. His story begins in one of the *worst* times in Israel's history— and when you remember that the Egyptians enslaved them before they wandered in the desert for forty years, that says a lot! The Bible sets the scene for the terrible ordeal experienced by the Hebrew people.

> The Israelites did evil in the eyes of the LORD, and for seven years he gave them into the hands of the Midianites. Because the power of Midian was so oppressive, the Israelites prepared shelters for themselves in mountain clefts, caves and strongholds. Whenever the Israelites planted their crops, the Midianites, Amalekites and other eastern peoples invaded the country. They camped on the land and ruined the crops all the way to Gaza and did not spare a living thing for Israel, neither sheep nor cattle nor donkeys. They came up with their livestock and their tents like swarms of locusts. It was impossible to count them or their camels; they invaded the land to ravage it. Midian so impoverished the Israelites that they cried out to the LORD for help.
>
> —JUDGES 6:1–6

Yet again, in order for His people to repent and return to Him, God allowed them to face the consequences of their sinfulness. This time He permitted the Midianites to conquer them for seven years, and not just the Midianites but a plague of enemies described here "like swarms of locusts." This forced the people of Israel to run and hide wherever they could take cover—caves, crevices, and caverns. Their enemies knew how to keep them weak too, because the Midianites and their fellow marauders would ravage the fields and farms of the Hebrew people, stealing or destroying all their food, livestock, and valuables. The Jewish people could barely get over one attack before another occurred.

God heard the desperate prayers of His people and decided to raise up a leader who would, with the Lord's help, defeat the Midianites. I cannot help but believe God has an incredible sense of humor because the young man He selected seemed to be the most unqualified around. Notice how Gideon himself pointed out his deficiencies right away.

> When the angel of the Lord appeared to Gideon, he said, "The Lord is with you, mighty warrior."
>
> "Pardon me, my lord," Gideon replied, "but if the Lord is with us, why has all this happened to us? Where are all his wonders that our ancestors told us about when they said, 'Did not the Lord bring us up out of Egypt?' But now the Lord has abandoned us and given us into the hand of Midian."
>
> The Lord turned to him and said, "Go in the strength you have and save Israel out of Midian's hand. Am I not sending you?"
>
> "Pardon me, my lord," Gideon replied, "but how can I save Israel? My clan is the weakest in Manasseh, and I am the least in my family."
>
> The Lord answered, "I will be with you, and you will strike down all the Midianites, leaving none alive."
>
> —Judges 6:12–16

The contrast between the Lord's message and Gideon's response could not be sharper. After seven long years of death, destruction, and destitution, God answered the prayers of His people and began by sharing the exciting news with Gideon. Right away Gideon appeared not only skeptical but downright sassy! In response he basically said, "Really? You talking to me? Uh, excuse me, but if you speak the truth, then why am I sitting here, hiding out and threshing wheat—work often done by the women around here?" Even after God's messenger reassured Gideon, he still had not convinced this young man! He replied, "But I am the runt of my family, which is from the weakest clan out of them all!"

Gideon could not imagine how God wanted to speak into his future. And it would take some major convincing.

But God took care of it.

God never abandons His people.

He has chosen you just as He chose Gideon.

FAITH OVER FEAR

God had His work cut out for Him with Gideon. The setting clearly reinforces the dire straits of the entire nation of Israel. Before this exchange with the angel, as Judges 6:11 tells us, Gideon threshed wheat in a winepress to hide it from the Midianites. He did not farm, fight, or forage for food with his father and brothers. And to top it all off Gideon does not even have the proper tools in the right setting, typically a mill or threshing floor. So no wonder he struggled to take this angel's greeting of "mighty warrior" seriously!

Before we are too hard on Gideon for doubting God's future for him, we might need to think about our own responses at times when God has revealed where He wants to take us. When we moved from Pennsylvania to California to start a new church, I struggled to believe God really wanted us to do it. His Spirit kept affirming it in my heart, and the details continued to unfold as well.

But still I wondered if I had what it takes. Maybe that vision I had as a teenager watching TV amounted to nothing more than wishful thinking. I knew God had called me to preach and pastor, but maybe He just wanted me to remain an associate pastor in a small church back East. Did God really intend for me to start a new church that might grow into a congregation of thousands of people? Did He really want me traveling and speaking before huge crowds? And what if He opened up a leadership position to help other churches and pastors, community leaders, or even elected officials?

Have you ever had a Gideon moment of your own? Maybe you had a sense of God calling you to do something, and yet you felt underprepared or ill-equipped to do the job. Perhaps you felt Him directing you to make a major move into a new role, and yet your circumstances seemed too overwhelming to overcome. You simply could not imagine how you would ever do what God seemed to be telling you to do.

Your mind of fear cannot produce a life of faith.

God's power overcomes inadequacy, inexperience, or insecurity, whether for Gideon or for people like you and me. God does not see our circumstances the way we do. We look around us as well as inside us, and we fail to recognize possibilities for His power, instead often focusing on our flaws, failures, and fears. Jesus said, "With man this is impossible, but with God all things are possible" (Matt. 19:26). Often we quickly limit what God wants to do in our future because we only believe what we see with our mortal eyes. We cannot see ourselves the way God sees us—as His mighty warriors—when we see ourselves as weak and scrawny.

Fortunately God's power includes the ability to help us see our future with an eternal perspective. He loves to remind us that our thoughts about ourselves do not limit us! No matter how we see ourselves—powerless, empty, sinful, scared, uneducated, underqualified—He only asks that we trust Him. With God on our side, who can be against us? We cannot be against ourselves and limit God's power in our lives if we simply trust Him and step out in faith.

Too often we allow our thoughts, perceptions, assumptions, and expectations to shackle us to what we perceive as absolute reality. We look for details and supporting evidence to reinforce what we believe, refusing to consider other possibilities—even of the supernatural kind. We know God can do anything—after all, He is God—but we cannot comprehend why He would choose us. And as a result we resist or outright refuse to move into our Father's future for us.

Instead we cling to our negative, past-focused point of view. We see ourselves as less than others, and therefore we cannot imagine how or even why God would choose to work through us. We think we do not come from a good family or have real ministry training. We have not studied the Bible enough or learned how to be a leader. We get in our own way when God wants to show us the mighty warrior He has made us to be.

When your mind focuses on your weakness, you cannot accept God's strength. If the man at Bethesda had not believed in the possibility of ever walking, then even after Jesus healed him, he could have refused to try to get on his feet. He could have said, "I have tried before many times, and it was impossible. I am and always will be an invalid, a paralytic, a man who cannot walk." Instead he received instant healing from his past way of seeing himself, and he dared to believe he could walk!

Your mind of fear cannot produce a life of faith.

Let go of who you once were so God can show you who you will become.

You are next to be God's mighty warrior…

…if you will get on your feet!

> **Because of who God is, you do not have to worry, wallow, or wonder about what you cannot do.**

Gideon struggled with the way he thought about himself. And as the Bible points out, our thoughts do have power: "For as he thinks in his heart, so is he" (Prov. 23:7, NKJV). Even when the angel of the Lord showed up there beneath the old oak tree, Gideon seemed remarkably reserved. Instead of getting excited about the opportunity ahead with God on his side, he could not get past his own paralysis. He not only doubted himself, but also he even apparently doubted God!

While feeling afraid does not mean you have sinned, you should not allow our fear to grow into the poison that paralyzes you and keeps you in the past. Everyone deals with fear from time to time. But if you allow it to control your life and keep you paralyzed, you risk missing out on the future God has for you. When Jesus tells you to walk, never allow fear to interrupt the miracle He wants to pour over you.

Always remember: you do not serve a God of fear but a God of love. You have a caring Father on your side. Because of who God is, you do not have to worry, wallow, or wonder about what you cannot do. His Word tells us, "For God has not given us a spirit of fear, but of power and of love and of a sound mind" (2 Tim. 1:7, NKJV). Lingering fearful thoughts that cloud your thinking and hinder your actions do not come from God. He never operates out of fear. Do not let the enemy use fear to block the path toward your divine destiny.

THE PROBLEM WITH *WHY*

Keep in mind that Gideon's fear did not disqualify him from being used by God. The Lord just had to break through those fears and help Gideon see himself differently. Similarly, God had not been sitting idly by, ignoring the cries of His own people. The Lord had His plan, and with Gideon selected, He could now begin.

Ironically Gideon's fearful thinking so enveloped him that he did not recognize God's answer to the Israelites' prayers! Remember, Gideon's immediate response questioned this delay by asking, "Why, Lord? Where is the God who set our people free from Egypt?" (Judg. 6:13, paraphrase). God had chosen Gideon as the leader to deliver His people just as God had chosen Moses to lead the exodus from Egypt. But Gideon could not see the forest for the trees! Or in his case, as we will explore in a moment, he could not see the forest for the fleece!

Gideon resisted God's future and lingered in the past, fixating on the problem of "Why?" God on the other hand arrived on the scene not to answer a man's "Why?" but to provide him with a "What?" Yes, Gideon's family background might have identified him as the weakest and the youngest, but he quickly used this as an excuse. Basically he dared to question God's choice—as if he knew better than God!

A large family, such as we see with the people of Israel, often considers the youngest weaker than the older siblings. In some cases the baby of the family might be spoiled and even feel entitled, such as we find in the story Jesus told about the prodigal son. So Gideon may have been conditioned to see himself as young and weak, unqualified and inexperienced, by his family, friends, and neighbors. But once again, it does not matter what others say about you—only what God says!

> We think that with all our past problems—poverty, probation, powerlessness—God cannot possibly choose us for a glorious future. My friend, do not believe that lie!

The fact that Gideon came from the weakest tribe may have been an economic factor as well as an emotional or physical one. Having little money might have forced him to thresh wheat with a wine press, a reminder of just how poor they were. We may use our own lack of resources as an excuse as well. We assume that because we are the first in our family to be a Christian, we cannot lead a large ministry. We believe that because we did not finish our degree, we cannot fulfill the potential we know God has placed inside us. We think that because our parents were not wealthy or influential, we will always be inferior to others.

We lock ourselves into faulty thinking without even realizing it. We assume that because our parents were not successful, we will not be either—or because they were always stressed out and lived paycheck to paycheck, we must inevitably live that way too. We think that with all our past problems—poverty, probation, powerlessness—God cannot possibly choose us for a glorious future.

My friend, do not believe that lie!

Your past does not determine your future. God does!

SHOW ME A SIGN

When we succumb to our doubts and insecurities, we sometimes need to be reassured. Like Gideon we want confirmation from God. But often in asking for this reassurance, we really just stall and find a way to extend our doubts. Gideon told the angel of the Lord, "Uh, if you really want to help me, then let me go make a meal for you, and when I come back, you will still be here." Gideon made the meal and returned. And guess what? The angel of the Lord had remained there (Judg. 6:17–21), yet Gideon was not convinced.

> Gideon said to God, "If you will save Israel by my hand as you have promised—look, I will place a wool fleece on the threshing floor. If there is dew only on the fleece and all the ground is dry, then I will know that you will save Israel by my hand, as you said." And that is what happened. Gideon rose early the next day; he squeezed the fleece and wrung out the dew—a bowlful of water.
>
> Then Gideon said to God, "Do not be angry with me. Let me make just one more request. Allow me one more test with the fleece, but this time make the fleece dry and let the ground be covered with dew." That night God did so. Only the fleece was dry; all the ground was covered with dew.
>
> —JUDGES 6:36–40

Gideon had to work through the process of allowing God to change his thought process. When our thinking focuses on the past, we need help getting a glimpse of our future. Fortunately God patiently transforms us, helping us see the truth. He never wants us to play games or try to manipulate Him, but He loves us enough to humor us in the midst of our foibles and frailties. For this reason He reminds us in His Word to focus not on our own thoughts and feelings but on His eternal truth: "Do not conform to the pattern of this world, but be transformed by the renewing of your mind. Then you will be able to test and approve what God's will is—his good, pleasing and perfect will" (Rom. 12:2).

When we allow God to renew our minds, He changes our thinking. We let Him do this by reading, studying, and meditating on His Word. We spend time in prayer and get to know Him more intimately, trusting Him as our loving Father. We obey Him and seek to please Him. We let go of our old way of doing things on our own and embrace God's way. The Bible tells us, "You were taught, with regard to your former way of life, to put off your old self, which is being corrupted by its deceitful desires; to be made new in the attitude of your minds; and to put on the new self, created to be like God in true righteousness and holiness" (Eph. 4:22–24).

I love Gideon's story because even in the midst of this young man's insecurities and warped thinking, God loved him enough to do as Gideon asked and make the future abundantly clear. God viewed the fleeces as unnecessary, but He nonetheless did as Gideon asked to help him see differently. God does not want to punish us for clinging to our past—He wants to love us into our future. I do not believe Gideon's requests upset or offended the Lord. Instead God wanted Gideon to trust Him—just as He still wants us to trust Him today.

God spoke truth and let its power permeate the way Gideon thought about himself and the future God called him to fulfill. In fact, the Lord called Gideon a mighty warrior.

> **God does not want to punish us for clinging to our past—He wants to love us into our future.**

The real test comes, of course, when we put our thoughts into action. Will we trust God enough to break away from the past and old ways in order to walk in faith and fight for our future? Once in hiding and fearful of danger, Gideon finally began to act on God's instruction. At first he gathered an army of thirty-two thousand men, but God said, "Too many." Instead God instructed His mighty warrior on how to distinguish the soldiers God wanted Gideon to take into battle with him. In the end only three hundred passed the test (Judg. 7:2–8).

Can you see the difference in action? Gideon went from thinking of himself as nothing, the weakest and scrawniest, to leading three hundred men to face an army of over one hundred thousand men. With the odds against him, Gideon now knew that God would fight for him! It did not matter how many soldiers he had because God would be on his side. The victory belongs to the Lord, and Him alone!

God then instructed Gideon to surround the Midianites while holding torches and horns—no fancy spears, arrows, or weapons, just a torch in one hand and a horn in the other! Gideon followed the instructions, and the Bible says that when the Hebrew army under Gideon's command blew the horns and held up the torches, the Midianites woke up, heard the commotion, and became so confused that they began killing each other! They basically defeated themselves thanks to the strategy God gave to Gideon. He and his three hundred men captured the remaining soldiers and secured the victory for Israel by relying on the Lord's power.

While he certainly witnessed a miraculous military victory, I believe Gideon won a far more miraculous battle inside his own mind and heart! Rescued from the paralysis of the past,

Gideon faced his fears with the help of God and overcame them, freeing him to fight for and win his future.

BACK TO THE FUTURE

Maybe you want to release the past and face your God-given future, but your fears continue to linger. You hear God calling you His mighty warrior, and you know He has the power to overcome any and all obstacles in your path. Still you wait and wonder and grow wishy-washy. You cannot figure out how everything will come together. You have no logical or rational explanation for what must take place to go forward, so you keep lying on the ground—no longer paralyzed but hesitant to test your new mobility.

We must realize that God still tells us today the same thing He told Gideon: "Go in the strength you have and save Israel out of Midian's hand. Am I not sending you?" (Judg. 6:14). We focus on all the reasons why this will not work when God insists on us trusting Him and going forward anyway. Basically the Lord tells us, "Just trust Me on this. Go with what you have, and I will take care of the rest. We got this!"

Even when we continue to make excuse after excuse, God washes them away like dew on a fleece! Remember what He told Gideon, His handpicked mighty warrior: "I will be with you, and you will strike down all the Midianites" (Judg. 6:16). By my count, God eventually told Gideon "Hey, I am with you!" three times. Then He even went so far as to tell Gideon exactly what would happen. God did not leave Gideon a victim of his past; God revealed his victorious future to him.

Nevertheless a battle ensued in Gideon's mind. Even though God had already shown him the victory, Gideon had to catch up in his ability to trust and act on his faith. Gideon's doubts led him to test God at least three times before God finally convinced Gideon He would be on his side.

We have to take every negative thought captive and demolish thoughts that are not of God. We have to train our mind to think through the lens of God's truth and not our own perceptions and assumptions.

We all have battles in our minds when we know that our thinking does not reflect God's perspective. At these times, we must claim the victory Christ has already won for us. We must declare our divine destiny and not the derailment of the devil. When negative, defeating, impure thoughts come into our minds, we must take them captive. We must pray and claim the victory we already have been given, reminding our enemy of the futility of his attempts. We can do all things through Jesus Christ who strengthens us and assures us that we have all we need.

It took a while, but Gideon finally started believing God's promises. Trusting God fully, Gideon went to battle against the Midianites, followed God's instructions, and defeated the enemy who had been terrorizing Israel for the past seven years. Similarly it may take us a while too before we can get up and walk, but we already possess the miracle.

My friend, do not allow circumstances, crisis conditions, or the critical concerns of others to leave you lying in the dust when God calls you to run in the sun. If you know you do not see yourself as God sees you, then take time to focus on His Word and learn the truth. You are a child of the King. You are

His beloved. You are forgiven in Christ Jesus. You are an heir of righteousness. You are an eternal citizen of heaven.

Let go of the past and step into your future.

Maybe you have been delayed, derailed, or discouraged, but the time has come to go back to your future.

Your future begins right now.

God does not want to renovate your past—He wants to release your future!

God has spoken into what lies ahead, and your old ways of thinking, seeing, and acting no longer have a hold on you. Start viewing yourself through God's eyes and not your own. Your future depends on it! What God does next in your life will break the rules of expectation and the norms of conformity and bypass your usual way of thinking.

Like the paralyzed man at Bethesda, when Jesus tells you to stand up and walk, you do not have time to come up with excuses! You must believe, my friend, that at long last...you are next!

Chapter Seven

YOU ARE NEXT...

AS GOD EMPOWERS YOU TO DO WHAT YOU COULD NOT DO BEFORE

God does not call those who have it all;
He calls those willing to surrender all.

I AM LIVING PROOF that God blesses us in our dependency on Him. This dependence on Him has been a challenging process, but it has been essential to enable me to do what I cannot do on my own.

You see, my path to leading the one of world's largest evangelical networks can be described only as orchestrated by God. I have always been passionate not only about my relationship with Jesus Christ and the Great Commission to share the good news of the gospel with the world but also about uniting multiethnic and multigenerational evangelical voices to make a difference in the quality of life for all people. I have always felt called to minister to both body and soul because I see the cross of Christ uniting heaven and earth, healing us both vertically in our relationship with God and horizontally in our relationships with one another. Jesus tells us He came to bring a full, abundant life (John 10:10), and I know God has called me to be a catalyst and facilitator of His power in the lives of others.

With a Spirit-fueled passion to reconcile Billy Graham's message of salvation through Christ with Dr. Martin Luther King Jr.'s march for justice, as I mentioned earlier, I endeavored to establish a movement with a goal of doing nothing less than changing the world.

THE PROBLEM WITH MY PROBLEM

Knowing and embracing God's calling to lead and serve this movement, I nonetheless made a crucial mistake. You would think that since I was a believer for decades as well as a pastor, I would know better than anyone what it means to rely on God.

And while I have always understood this need cognitively, it took some humbling experiences for me to realize that I had faltered, fallen, and failed to accomplish my God-given mission because I depended on others and myself more than I depended on God.

I can see in hindsight how I unintentionally kept my impact paralyzed by trying to carry the movement through my own power. Without recognizing my self-sufficiency and autonomous control, I worked hard to sustain and spread the mission, ministry, and mandate all by myself. I traveled and networked all the time, I raised funds all the time, and I rarely turned down an opportunity to speak, teach, or preach. In my mind at the time, I had done the hard work necessary for the movement to survive and thrive.

Like the man at the pool of Bethesda, though, I did not get very far.

STEP BACK OR STEP UP

Then it happened—that moment, that precise encounter when your life gets shaken by a truth that will define you forever. I remember praying and asking God, "Why?" And then I was filled with the Holy Spirit, and God gave me a simple rubric that changed my life and the trajectory of our movement from that moment on. "Live a holy, healed, healthy, happy, humble, hungry, honoring life, and change the world!"

Wow! I got it. It is not about me. It is not about my ability; it is about His anointing. It is not about my potential; it is about His power. It is not about what I do for God; it is about what God already did for me. It is not about my fortitude; it is about

His favor. It is not about me. It is not about me. It is not about me. It truly is about Him—not just rhetorically but in action, word, deed, and thought. It is all about Jesus.

And as I acknowledged this truth, the NHCLC began to explode! As if to underline the lesson He wanted me to learn, God blessed our organization and my leadership in so many directions. Unsolicited donations came in as new contributors, sponsors, and ministry partners asked to fund our endeavors. Unexpected invitations opened up and provided platforms far more significant than any I had ever attained in my past efforts. Top news media began covering us front and center, seeking me out to comment on matters of faith, culture, and public policy.

The more I stopped working through my own efforts and simply relied on God, the more He blessed me and the impact of the NHCLC. For example, in January 2013 I became the first Latino ever to deliver the keynote address at the Martin Luther King Jr. Annual Commemorative Service held at Ebenezer Baptist Church in Atlanta, Georgia. That same year, I accepted an invitation to give the keynote address at the Ethics and Public Policy Center's National Religious Freedom Conference in Washington, DC. I have had other unbelievably prestigious opportunities to speak—at Princeton, Yale, Promise Keepers, Liberty University, the National Association of Evangelicals, and the White House.

In fact, the White House not only invited me to speak but also to meet with then-President George W. Bush. After President Obama was elected, he asked me to serve on his White House Task Force on Fatherhood and Healthy Families. Other leaders and members of Congress actively sought out my views and insight on issues and policy objectives. In 2016 I accepted an invitation to pray from the presidential podium as part of the inauguration ceremony of Donald J. Trump.

Today the NHCLC has been recognized by the *New York Times*, the *Wall Street Journal*, *Christianity Today*, *Charisma* magazine, NBC, Telemundo, Univision, Fox News, CNN, and a number of additional media outlets, publications, and periodicals as America's largest and most influential Hispanic and Latino Christian organization with over forty thousand certified member churches in the United States. We join in covenant relationship with ministries and churches in Latin America and around the world.

My friend, I share all this with you not to brag at all, so forgive me if this comes across as immodest. Because I intend to show you just the opposite—how I could never have made any of this happen! Only God could bring about so many incredible blessings, opportunities, and accolades. Only God could open the doors to the White House for a geeky, *Star Trek*–loving Puerto Rican like myself.

As soon as I stepped back and surrendered my control to God's sovereignty, He resuscitated our organization and began working through it in miraculous ways—for His glory and His kingdom!

When I stepped back, God stepped up.

SINK OR SWIM

Can you relate to my experience? Have you ever tried so hard to make something work, maybe even something you knew God wanted you to do, only to have it fail? As we see throughout the

Bible, God wants His children to rely on Him. He knows the best plan for us, and He knows how we often get into trouble when we become self-sufficient and think we can accomplish what only He can do.

Sometimes when we have tried and tried to stand on our own two feet only to fall time and time again, we quit trying. We assume we will always remain on the ground, so why torture ourselves with false hope? I wonder if the paralyzed man felt that way that day beside the temple pool at Bethesda. Perhaps you and I might be tempted to hesitate and think about the likelihood that our next attempt would be unsuccessful since all the ones preceding it have failed.

But apparently the man did not try to think about what Jesus commanded him to do—he just did it! "Then Jesus said to him, 'Get up! Pick up your mat and walk.' At once the man was cured; he picked up his mat and walked" (John 5:8–9). Notice it says, "At once"! Not after a few minutes, not after he had explained to Jesus why it would not work, not after he changed sandals and felt better about how he looked!

At once!

When Jesus told him to stand up, He did not use just any old phrase. He did not ask a question or issue a request. Jesus' words imperatively instructed the man to do what he could not do before.

An encounter with Jesus through the power of the Holy Spirit will always empower you to do what you could not do before. One moment you cannot walk, and the next moment you can. When Jesus shows up, He immediately empowers you to do what you could not do before.

Unlike the man at Bethesda, however, we often allow our fears to overwhelm our faith. Instead of getting up at once, we hesitate and leave the door open for our fears to take over. I began serving and leading the NHCLC not in my own power but through God's power. But then I started to think I had to do it myself; I held myself responsible for whether we would sink or swim. I became so determined for the organization to succeed that I left God out of the equation. I knew I needed His power, but I did not rely on it daily, hourly, minute by minute.

> **An encounter with Jesus through the power of the Holy Spirit will always empower you to do what you could not do before.**

In those situations when our fear undermines our faith, we would do well to remember the example of one of my favorite disciples, Simon Peter. I am not sure if any follower of Jesus went through more ups and downs than this passionate fisherman who clearly loved the Lord but also battled personal fears to which we can all relate. In one of their most dramatic encounters, notice what happens when Peter quit walking by faith and instead relied on his own ability.

> Shortly before dawn Jesus went out to them, walking on the lake. When the disciples saw him walking on the lake, they were terrified. "It's a ghost," they said, and cried out in fear.
>
> But Jesus immediately said to them: "Take courage! It is I. Do not be afraid."

"Lord, if it's you," Peter replied, "tell me to come to you on the water."

"Come," he said.

Then Peter got down out of the boat, walked on the water and came toward Jesus. But when he saw the wind, he was afraid and, beginning to sink, cried out, "Lord, save me!"

Immediately Jesus reached out his hand and caught him. "You of little faith," he said, "why did you doubt?"

—Matthew 14:25–31

STANDING IN THE STORM

This scene took place after Jesus fed the five thousand by blessing the bread-and-fish lunch of one little boy (Matt. 14:13–21; John 6:5–13). He then sent the disciples by boat to the other side of the lake while He dismissed the crowd and took some time to be alone with God (Matt. 14:22–23). In the meantime the disciples were taking a boat across the lake in the middle of the night when a storm blew in.

As if being in the middle of a storm in open water in the dark did not seem spooky enough, then the disciples looked up and saw a man coming toward them—walking on the surface of the choppy water! Because the Gospel writer tells us it was Jesus before the disciples recognized their Master, we might be tempted to laugh at their hasty, imaginative conclusion. But in all honesty we all tend to allow our fears to jump ahead of our faith at times.

And the disciples did precisely that. They assumed it must be a ghost coming toward them because who or what else could walk on water? So Jesus identified Himself and reassured His friends. While they must not have seen their Master walk on water before, they had surely seen Him do enough miraculous, unimaginable feats not to question His ability to do something like this. After all, had they not just witnessed Him taking a meager meal of five loaves and two fish, blessing it, and transforming it into more Filet-O-Fish sandwiches than McDonald's has ever served?

Like us at times, however, the disciples were skeptical. Peter, much like our friend Gideon setting out his fleeces, wanted some evidence to back up the ghostly stranger's claim. And do not you just love the proof Peter asked for? "If that is really You, Lord," he said, "then let me do what You are doing! Let me walk on water just like You are doing."

Now, this request to you or I might have been met with the same kind of response I used to give my kids when they asked me if they could keep another stray kitten or puppy. "I do not think that is a very good idea," I would say as kindly and gently as possible while internally thinking, "No way are we keeping that critter!"

Instead Jesus simply said, "Come."

I am struck by the similarity in many ways to His instruction to the man who could not walk. "Get up!" the Lord said. "Walk toward Me! Come on!" Peter did as he was instructed, getting out of the boat and walking on water just like his Master! But notice what happened next: "When he saw the wind, he was afraid and, beginning to sink, cried out, 'Lord, save me!'" (v. 30).

How many times have you obeyed God's call on your life and started to do what you could never have imagined yourself doing? How many times have you stepped out of your comfort zone, your boat of security, and started to walk by faith toward the Master's voice? Maybe it surprises you just as much as everyone else around you. They did not think you could do it, and like our old friend Gideon from the previous chapter, maybe you did not think you could do it either. But now look at you—doing what has never been done, walking on water!

But not for long.

Like Peter, the winds of life startle us and shake our faith.

We look down and cannot believe the water's surface supports our feet. We look up and see the rain falling and the clouds gathering as we hear the wind howling. Not only do we have the ability to do the impossible, walk on water, but suddenly we realize we can do it in the midst of a storm, which surely must be even more impossible—as if degrees of impossibility exist! This only goes to show the way we get in our heads and try to conform God's power to our understanding of the world around us.

Just think about what it would have been like if the man at Bethesda had acted like this or behaved like Peter. There he is, lying on the ground for thirty-eight years, when along comes Jesus, who tells him to get to his feet, pick up his mat, and walk. So the man stands and takes a step on legs that have not known smooth, fluid motion like this in nearly four decades. Then he hesitates. He looks down. No, this cannot be happening! Those are not his feet, are they? They seem to be moving just fine, and they feel great, better than ever before, but that doesn't seem possible, does it? After all, he is paralyzed. He cannot be walking around like someone on a Sunday stroll through the park!

We all have moments, like Peter, when we shift our focus from Jesus to our own ability—or lack thereof—to do what

He has instructed us to do. We allow our fears to overwhelm us, our logic to overtake us, and our doubts to overpower us. Immediately we begin sinking! We cannot keep going. We know we cannot do the impossible—and apparently we are not sure God can either. But He is God, after all, so we cry out, "Lord! Save me!"

> **When you try to walk in your own power, you will fall, no matter how many times you try, no matter how much effort you expend.**

Jesus extends His hand and catches us, just as He caught Peter in that frightful moment. But the Lord also reminds us with the same words He told His disciple: "You of little faith, why did you doubt?" (v. 31).

When you try to walk in your own power, you will fall, no matter how many times you try, no matter how much effort you expend. But when you look at Jesus and draw your power from Him, then you can do what you could not do before. Like Peter, you can walk on water. Like the paralyzed man, you can walk by faith.

BREAKFAST ON THE BEACH

Peter intrigues me because this incident on the lake was not his only time to slip and sink when relying on his own power. You might recall that later Peter, along with other disciples, accompanied Jesus to the Garden of Gethsemane to keep vigil in prayer prior to Jesus' arrest, crucifixion, and death. At that time Peter had grown so committed to his Master, he even drew his sword and cut off the ear of the high priest's servant, who was part of the group there to arrest Christ (John 18:10).

Within a matter of mere hours, however, this same brawny, zealous defender of Jesus claimed that he did not know the carpenter from Nazareth at all! When others challenged his denial, Peter repeated his lie two more times (Luke 22:54–62), unintentionally fulfilling the prophetic warning that the Lord Himself had given Peter (Matt. 26:34). I find it hard not to see Peter once again looking into the face of the wind, fearing the storm, and sinking in place. Instead of focusing on Jesus, Peter reacted out of fear and assumed control. "I better lie about knowing Jesus or they will arrest me too!" he might have been thinking. Instead of trusting God for his safety, Peter tried to take control.

Peter's story was not over, though. Just as Jesus reached out and saved him from sinking in the storm, the Lord showed Peter His forgiveness in a particularly personal, poignant way. After His resurrection Christ appeared at various times and places to His followers. While each encounter was indeed memorable, I cannot help but believe this scene of breakfast on the beach had the most profound effect on Peter.

> Early in the morning, Jesus stood on the shore, but the disciples did not realize that it was Jesus.
>
> He called out to them, "Friends, haven't you any fish?"
> "No," they answered.
> He said, "Throw your net on the right side of the boat and you will find some." When they did, they were unable to haul the net in because of the large number of fish.

Then the disciple whom Jesus loved said to Peter, "It is the Lord!" As soon as Simon Peter heard him say, "It is the Lord," he wrapped his outer garment around him (for he had taken it off) and jumped into the water. The other disciples followed in the boat, towing the net full of fish, for they were not far from shore, about a hundred yards. When they landed, they saw a fire of burning coals there with fish on it, and some bread.

—John 21:4–9

The disciples were fishing but, as Jesus pointed out, not on the right side! When we cast our nets where we think we can attain what we want, we usually end up empty-handed. Only when we obey our Master's instruction can we do what we could not do before.

Not only did Jesus cook breakfast for Peter and the others, but the Lord had already also delivered prophetic words of grace to the fisherman as well: "And I tell you, you are Peter, and on this rock I will build my church, and the gates of hell shall not prevail against it" (Matt. 16:18, esv). Christ never gave up on His friend and pushed through Peter's fears to uncover his faith. Jesus wanted to work through Peter's life and transform His follower's passion into precision. After Jesus ascended, Peter spent the rest of his life preaching and spreading the news of the gospel wherever he went, eventually being martyred for his faith. He no longer feared the storms of life but trusted God to be with him in the midst of them.

Peter grew from the kind of person who knew he could never walk on water in his own power to one who continually stepped out in faith to share Christ with others. Peter went from a man who denied knowing Jesus three times to one willing to face death for his beloved Savior. Peter knew firsthand that encountering the love of Jesus and the power of the Holy Spirit will radically empower us to do what we could not do before. He exemplified living proof of the truth Paul wrote: "Anyone who belongs to Christ has become a new person. The old life is gone; a new life has begun!" (2 Cor. 5:17, NLT).

RISE UP

My friend, you may not believe you have the same faith as Peter, but you do. You might not feel as able to leap to your feet as the man at Bethesda, but you can. You might not want to try once again to do what you have not been able to do before, but you must. Because when you encounter the presence of the living God in your life, you can do what you could not do before. All who encounter Jesus and invite His Spirit into their lives experience an abundance of power that enables them to exceed anything they have ever done before. Jesus said, "With man this is impossible, but with God all things are possible" (Matt. 19:26).

How many times did the man at Bethesda try to stand up with his own strength and fail?
How many times did he depend on others to get him to his miracle and fail?
How many times did he lament not having what others had?

Then all of a sudden Jesus showed up, and the miracle began! And it started not with Jesus' command to walk but with the diagnostic question of the great physician. Whatever else you do with this man's story of complete and total healing, don't you dare forget Jesus' first question to him: "Do you want to get well?"

It was not an insult, not an obvious query, and not a rhetorical question—but an invitation. Before you obey Jesus' command to stand and walk, you must answer this question openly and honestly. Do you want to quit making excuses? Do you want to stop playing the victim? Do you want to end the blame game? Do you want to be made whole?

Do you want to get well?

It is very simple, and yet we often complicate it. We fear letting go and letting God empower us. The uncertainty of who we will be without our paralysis scares us.

The amazing Christian writer C. S. Lewis captured the fear of this decision so perfectly in his book *The Great Divorce*. In his allegorical story a group of people travel through the foothills of heaven on their way to hell. These travelers appear ghostlike, insubstantial, and fragile as they cling to their own sinful comforts and conveniences. One ghost passenger in particular has a red lizard, symbolizing the power of sin in his life, on his shoulder, constantly whispering in his ear. As the group nears heaven, an angel addresses this ghost and gives him an invitation to break the power of sin over his life so that God can transform it into something glorious.

As the angel and the ghost converse, the ghost with his lizard makes excuse after excuse why they do not want to part. The angel persists in the offer, however, until finally the ghost realizes how miserable the lizard-like hold of sin has made him. So the ghost asks the angel to remove the lizard, to destroy its power over him, which the angel proceeds to do. The pain feels agonizing and unbearable at the moment, but then a mighty transformation occurs. The ghost suddenly solidifies and becomes a man—and the remains of the lizard become a beautiful, lively horse with a golden mane. The man, who is now free from the lizard and the tormenting power of sin, climbs onto the horse and rides off toward heaven "like a shooting star."[1]

"Do you want to get well?" Jesus continues to ask. And contained within His words, we also find other invitations to the abundant life God wants to give us through His healing power:

> Do you want to do the impossible?
> Do you want to overcome your fears?
> Do you want to quit trying—and failing—in your own power?
> Do you want to fulfill the purpose for which God made you?
> Do you want to walk on water?
> Do you want to walk by faith?

Then get up! Stand up! Rise up! Through the power of Jesus Christ get up and do what you could not do before in your own strength; what you failed to do before because others abandoned you or failed you; what you were unable to do before because just like the man at Bethesda you depended on others more than you depended on God.

In Christ your areas of past failure will emerge as the arenas of your greatest success. Where you once strived and struggled, you will sail and saunter. Where you once labored in vain for temporary gain, you will now serve God's eternal kingdom with your unique purpose through the power of the Holy Spirit. You need not doubt the difference you make in this world because you know that God has equipped you for His righteous purpose to do what you could never do on your own. You need not labor in vain and hit your head against the wall because you do not seem to make any progress. You need not exhaust yourself by trying harder and exerting more force.

> **In Christ your areas of past failure will emerge as the arenas of your greatest success.**

You need only to surrender your control. Let go of the past and walk into the future. Get off the ground and get on your feet. I may never meet you in person, know your name, or shake your hand, but right now, as you read the words on this page, I prophetically declare:

> You will do what you could not do before!
> Your paralysis ends right here and right now, forever!

Not only will you never be paralyzed again, but from this moment on:

> You and your family will see what you could not see before.
> You and your family will achieve what you could not achieve before.

You and your family will accomplish what you could not accomplish before.

You and your family will occupy what you could not occupy before.

You and your family will conquer what you could not conquer before.

Stand up and be more than what you can ever be in your own power:

Stand up and be holy (1 Pet. 1:16).

Stand up and be one (John 17:21).

Stand up and be light (Matt. 5:14).

Stand up and be filled with the Holy Spirit (Eph. 5:18).

Your paralysis has ended.

Your faith will never be paralyzed again!

Your family will never be paralyzed again!

Your favor will never be paralyzed again!

Your children and your children's children will not be paralyzed!

My friend, do you want to do what you could not do before? You are next!

Chapter Eight

YOU ARE NEXT...

TO PICK UP YOUR MAT

It is not only what we do, but
also what we do not do, for
which we are accountable.
—MOLIÈRE

I HATE MOVING.

As you might have guessed by now, I like initiative, efficiency, and organization in others and certainly in my own life. Moving from one household to another inherently undermines those practices at every turn. With my schedule before me, I can choose what gets on my calendar, when to slot it, and what to turn down. I can pray and read the Word and follow God's guidance about how I prioritize my time, seeking to be a good steward and doing what He wants me to do each day. But with moving, especially from one side of the country to the other as we did when we left Pennsylvania for California, so many variables spin out of control. My wife, Eva, and I make a fantastic team, and we both appreciate how well we work together. She knows I value productivity, and she does an amazing job getting things done and keeping our household running smoothly. And while we both begin the process of a move with a detailed timeline, endless lists, and an arsenal of packing supplies, we inevitably feel as if we have lost the battle.

Our last move spanned the shortest distance but felt the hardest. Maybe I am getting older and more "set in my ways," as my father used to say about himself, but this last time I became more and more impatient with the moving process.

First we began the purging process and coming to terms with how much stuff we needed to get rid of—everything from our kids' baby clothes and favorite toys to that broken smoothie machine someone gave us for Christmas last year to that baby jogger we used decades ago when our children were small. Then we went through the books and camping equipment.

As much as I tried to be ruthless about throwing things away, giving things away, and putting things away, I struggled as much as anyone with the flood of memories attached to specific items: a high school yearbook, the suit I wore when I preached my first sermon, the crystal platter—now cracked— we received as a wedding gift from a beloved aunt and uncle. If I am not careful, packing up my home office ends up taking twice as long as I planned. And the slower I pack, the more likely I am to keep things I really do not need to keep.

I do not merely want to own few belongings and organize my home life more efficiently; I believe how I handle material possessions reflects my relationship with God. When I get wrapped up in stuff, I find it easy to inadvertently give possessions and their acquisition more attention than I give the Lord. I would never intentionally create idols out of my numerous pairs of running shoes, a new set of golf clubs, or a Swiss-made diver's watch, but when they take up space inside me that I want God and only God to occupy, well, "Houston, we have a problem."

Please do not get me wrong—I am not saying that owning or enjoying possessions makes a person less spiritual. All good things come from God, and He blesses most of us with an abundance of all we need and more. It is simply that I do not want to rely on anything to give my soul life except the Spirit of the living God. I do not want to cling to any object that prevents me from stepping out in faith when I hear the voice of Jesus saying, "Get up! Pick up your mat and walk!"

SOUVENIRS OF SUFFERING

I wonder how long the man lying there beside the pool of Bethesda had been carrying his mat. John 5:5 tells us he had been an invalid for thirty-eight years, so I wonder if he had been carrying around the same mat for that long. It would not surprise me if, impoverished and uncared for throughout his entire life, he dragged around the same mat as a kind of security blanket—like Linus carries in his interactions with Snoopy and Charlie Brown in the *Peanuts* cartoons.

After nearly forty years the man's mat would have been tattered and threadbare, dirty and dusty. He may have hated his mat, viewing its necessity as a symbol of his own infirmity that required a cushion while reclining on the hard ground for most of the day. But he may have also loved it, regarding his mat as a souvenir of the suffering he endured for most of his life, a familiar comfort to soften the discomfort and discouragement of his disease.

We all have our mats—those possessions, souvenirs, reminders, and remnants of our ordeals and disorders—do we not? In many cases we cling to them because they have identified us to ourselves and others for much of our lives. The scar from the childhood surgery that left us self-conscious and insecure. The cane or walker we need to assist us in our ambulatory ambitions from one place to another. The pain medication that helped us endure the excruciating ordeal of our surgery after the accident, medication that we have come to rely on long after our bodies have healed.

Many people create a mat from items and objects that help them compensate for their personal insecurities and infirmities.

I know so many people living in mansions and driving beautiful luxury cars who grew up in the clutches of deprivation. They swore that someday they would escape the paralysis of their poverty and never know the shame of being homeless or the pangs of hunger, so they accumulate money and fine possessions as their mats—security blankets to insulate them from the pain of the past.

Other people cling to mats of their own making that symbolize their success and self-worth. For some it might be jewelry—a Rolex watch or diamond stud earrings; for others it might be designer clothing or a Louis Vuitton bag. Regardless of the objects, people take them wherever they go, reminding others of who they are—or who they want others to *think* they are. This kind of mat might feel like their security blanket, but others often see these items as "insecurity blankets"—indicators of status used to compensate for someone's self-doubts and insecurities.

Even not having a mat can become a kind of mat! Lately I have been fascinated at the way not having a lot of stuff has become a badge of honor for some people. An entire movement, generally known as minimalism, has been devoted to eliminating clutter and editing possessions down to a bare minimum. This trend toward decluttering and downsizing our possessions continues to emerge online, especially in social media, popular podcasts, personal blogs, and lifestyle sites. *The Life-Changing Magic of Tidying Up* by Marie Kondo, first published in Japanese in 2011 and in English in 2014, still pops up on best-seller lists, having sold millions of copies and spawning numerous similar books and lifestyle gurus.

Perhaps it makes sense that minimalism offers itself as a kind of antidote to the poison of prosperous paralysis often plaguing millions of people. When you consider the number of storage unit sites that continue to mushroom across the country, perhaps minimalism seeks to swing the pendulum of popular culture in the opposite direction. In fact, in a recent *New York Times* magazine article, writer Kyle Chayka explains, "Part pop philosophy and part aesthetic, minimalism presents a cure-all for a certain sense of capitalist overindulgence."[1]

But in many ways minimalism ironically seems to be just as trendy as collecting designer purses. Some people do not seem interested in letting go of their stuff as much as they want to be at the center of the latest hip trend in our culture right now. Last year everyone owned an enormous house; this year they all want to scale back to a tiny, environmentally friendly dwelling. Nonetheless, this still amounts to following trends instead of following Jesus.

They may have let go of their mat and sold it in a yard sale, but now the fact that they do not have a mat has become their mat! They take pride in the fact that they consider themselves just as cool as some people and cooler than others. Their identity becomes contingent on the absence of possessions in their lives, not their accumulation. Anything we let get in the way of our relationship with God becomes an idol. Idols usually grow into addictions.

Idols and addictions do not necessarily depend on tangible objects or material items. Many people who do not seem to have a physical mat to carry around often lug an invisible mat woven from the threads of their own attitudes, emotions, insecurities, and entitlement. Their past crises, wounds, traumas, and scars accumulate into a mat as unique and distinctive as our individual fingerprints. Instead of taking responsibility for their choices, these mats become a glue trap for the excuses, justifications, and personal loopholes they create for themselves.

WELCOME MAT OR MINEFIELD

As a third-generation Latino from a middle-class family in the working-class suburbs of the former Steel Belt, I witnessed so many people transform the pain of prejudice and the injury of injustice into their personal mat. These people's mats of anger, anxiety, and absorption simmer just below the surface. They use their mat as both shield and sword, a mask as well as a mirror, a welcome mat in a minefield, constantly defending and sustaining their own personal paralysis.

Having faced bullies and bias myself, I know the temptation to become a victim based on your demographic profile. You may not see yourself as a victim, but you use your status as a trump card in the game of life. Because our culture stereotypes so many people based on gender, race, ethnic background, economic status, and education level, you attempt to use the perceptions of others to your own advantage, inadvertently perpetuating the very stereotype you despise.

Sometimes the mat we must pick up goes to the core of our identity. As we have discussed, we can be tempted to cling to our past, to false labels based on what others think of us or who they want us to be. We easily remain in our paralysis and hug our mats as a kind of security blanket. But if we intend to move toward what God has for us, we must learn to travel light. We must let go of old loyalties that no longer serve us. We must embrace the journey of faith that God asks us to take.

> I know the temptation to become a victim based on your demographic profile. You may not see yourself as a victim, but you use your status as a trump card in the game of life.

One such sojourner called by God to walk in a different direction intrigues me: Rahab, the prostitute whose legacy of faithfulness eventually led to the birth line of Jesus Christ. Even the way Scripture refers to her denotes who she used to be before surrendering to God and choosing to serve Him. Rahab faced a choice between a past complacency facing destruction and a new future fueled entirely by faith. As the Israelites prepare to conquer Jericho, the city where she lived, Rahab had no time to deliberate.

> Then Joshua son of Nun secretly sent two spies from Shittim. "Go, look over the land," he said, "especially Jericho." So they went and entered the house of a prostitute named Rahab and stayed there.
>
> The king of Jericho was told, "Look, some of the Israelites have come here tonight to spy out the land." So the king of Jericho sent this message to Rahab: "Bring out the men who came to you and entered your house, because they have come to spy out the whole land."

But the woman had taken the two men and hidden them. She said, "Yes, the men came to me, but I did not know where they had come from. At dusk, when it was time to close the city gate, they left. I don't know which way they went. Go after them quickly. You may catch up with them." (But she had taken them up to the roof and hidden them under the stalks of flax she had laid out on the roof.) So the men set out in pursuit of the spies on the road that leads to the fords of the Jordan, and as soon as the pursuers had gone out, the gate was shut.

—JOSHUA 2:1–7

COURAGE IN A RED CORD

In a dramatic scene straight out of your favorite spy show or espionage movie, Rahab acted quickly and decisively. In a matter of mere moments, Rahab had to decide whether she would trust these foreigners who claimed they would conquer and destroy her hometown. Shrewd and savvy, Rahab struck a deal: she would help them as long as they saved her and her family during their siege (vv. 12–13). She acknowledged that she had heard about them and their God, how He delivered them from Egypt and parted the sea so they could escape Pharaoh's army.

But we must not overlook the fact that to strike this deal, something more than self-preservation motivated Rahab. She basically betrayed her friends, neighbors, and clients. She chose to place her faith in the God of the Hebrews rather than the idols worshipped in Jericho. She decided to give up her profession and go with strangers upon whom she would be reliant for her survival and that of her family. In other words, Rahab demonstrated unparalleled courage in picking up her mat!

Also, please do not miss that God selected Rahab just as He chooses each and every one of us for His glory and power to shine through us as we impact and advance His kingdom. Out of all the individuals to whom God could have led His spies, He picked a prostitute. He could have chosen a wealthy man, an innocent child, or an upstanding lady from a powerful family. God could have chosen a soldier, a carpenter, a merchant, a teacher, or even the king of Jericho. Instead God chose a woman whom most people probably despised and held in contempt.

The Bible not only identifies her as someone who had been a prostitute in her past, it equates her name with her profession. She worked as a prostitute still, allowing men to objectify her, use her body, and pay her money when God directed His spies to hide out in her home. And this non-Jewish woman— undoubtedly looked down upon by many Jews at the time— deceived the king's soldiers in order to save these strangers' lives and advance their plan for domination.

I love the way God gave Rahab a choice just as Jesus gave the man at Bethesda a choice: Do you want to get well? And instead of picking up her mat, Rahab picked up the scarlet cord the spies had instructed her to hang from her window as a sign to spare her household during the Israeli assault (v. 18). No longer would she be who she had been. The moment she hung that red rope from the top of her house, Rahab chose to walk by faith into her future.

Because of her faith, this lowliest of the low, a non-Jewish prostitute, received the blessing of the Lord. God saw her future, not her past. He looked at her heart, not her reputation. He offered the choice of life versus death. Like so many of the underdogs within the pages of the Bible, Rahab reminds us that no matter who we are or what we have done, if we will trust Him, God will save us. He will heal us and empower us to let go of the mats we once used and instead follow Him by faith.

FROM CRUTCH TO CROSS

Rahab also reminds us that even when our past reputation continues to follow us, we can still be redeemed and used by God. She went from being someone most people loathed to a heroine lauded in the pages of God's Word. Her past way of life, while still part of how others saw her and identified her, did not prevent her from becoming who God made her to be. For in the genealogy of Jesus at the beginning of his Gospel, Matthew identifies Rahab as the wife of Salmon and the mother of Boaz. And Boaz, you might recall, married another amazing woman of faith, Ruth.

Curiously enough, though, the other two references to Rahab in the New Testament include her old identifier.

> By faith the prostitute Rahab, because she welcomed the spies, was not killed with those who were disobedient.
> —HEBREWS 11:31

> In the same way, was not even Rahab the prostitute considered righteous for what she did when she gave lodging to the spies and sent them off in a different direction?
> —JAMES 2:25

Even for writers of Scripture the former label Rahab once had in Jericho continued to stick to her like gum on a shoe. But I do not believe Paul and James identify her this way out of carelessness or disrespect to her or other women. I am convinced they refer to her as a prostitute to highlight the contrast between who she had once been and who she became by following God. Rahab became a trophy of God's grace as He used her weakness to manifest His strength.

> God loves to shatter stereotypes and reverse our expectations.

Her legacy calls to mind Paul's words as he struggled with "a thorn in my flesh," as he called it (2 Cor. 12:7).

> Three times I pleaded with the Lord to take it away from me. But he said to me, "My grace is sufficient for you, for my power is made perfect in weakness." Therefore I will boast all the more gladly about my weaknesses, so that Christ's power may rest on me. That is why, for Christ's sake, I delight in weaknesses, in insults, in hardships, in persecutions, in difficulties. For when I am weak, then I am strong.
>
> —2 Corinthians 12:8–10

God loves to shatter stereotypes and reverse our expectations. As we have seen with so many people in the Bible—Abraham, Jacob, Gideon, Rahab, Paul, and the paralyzed man at Bethesda—the Lord delights in allowing His eternal light to shine through the cracks caused by our brokenness. Feeling paralyzed and shattered by circumstances can make us feel unfit to be used by God. But nothing we have done or can do disqualifies us from the love, grace, and power we have through Jesus Christ!

When we pick up our mats, we demonstrate our faith that despite who we once were, despite who others think we still are, despite our own fears and insecurities, we will no longer wallow in our past. Instead we will rise up and walk strong in the Lord! Our mats, which we once considered souvenirs of our suffering, have become trophies of grace, allowing others to see God do the impossible. The crutches we once clung to now become the crosses we bear as we become more like Christ. Through the power of His Spirit we walk upright in strength with a divine purpose to fulfill.

> We are no longer broken—we are whole!
> We are no longer prostitutes—we are precious!
> We are no longer mercenaries—we are bearers of mercy!
> We are no longer invalids—we are invincible!

YOUR MAT, HIS MASTERPIECE

I realize you will rarely find it easy to pick up your mat and refuse to rely on it as you once did. Picking up your mat means picking up after yourself and facing the consequences of past decisions. It means taking responsibility for your life instead of blaming others or waiting for someone to come through for you the way you have always wanted. If we want God to transform our mats into His masterpieces, we must master the pieces!

As you rise to your feet and consider your journey of faith, it may be tempting to think, "If I pick it up and start walking, those who knew me before might recognize the mat and assume that one day I will go back to it! If I carry it with me while I am walking, then I might be tempted to throw it down and collapse on the ground again. As hard as it seems to imagine, I might grow so weary of walking that I long for the days when I was paralyzed and could throw my mat down and lie on the ground." Like the people of Israel delivered from slavery in Egypt who hated wandering through the desert in pursuit of the Promised Land, we might become so uncomfortable depending on God's power and not our own that we complain and think we want to go back.

My friend, we must all learn to do one thing: pick up our mats! When you pick up your mat, you tell both heaven and hell and the people on earth that you do not live in the past anymore.

When you pick up your mat, you bring closure to the chapter of paralysis in your life. When you pick up your mat, you say that you no longer need this pallet of paralysis. Like discarded junk from the back of your spiritual storage unit, you have no need to save it!

> **When you pick up your mat, you tell both heaven and hell and the people on earth that you do not live in the past anymore.**

When you pick up your mat, you say, "I am no longer an invalid. I am no longer paralyzed. I am no longer trapped by my circumstances. That no longer defines me or describes me. I am not going to live there, and I am not going back there ever again." Instead we wear the garment of praise formed by the celebration of our healing. We revel in the revelation of our redemption, the fulfillment of the promise God makes to us in His Word: "This means that anyone who belongs to Christ has become a new person. The old life is gone; a new life has begun!" (2 Cor. 5:17, NLT).

Jesus asks us if we want to get well. Then He tells us to stand up, pick up our mat, and walk. While we instantaneously receive freedom, salvation, and restoration, we begin a journey of walking not by sight but by faith, not in our own power but in the power of the Holy Spirit within us. We have not attained perfection like Christ yet, and we have not completed our time here on earth.

We have work to do, a divine purpose to fulfill, and a race to run toward the eternal reward awaiting us with God in heaven. Many times we see Paul describe this journey of faith as a process in his letters to other believers: "Of course, my friends, I really do not think that I have already won it; the one thing I do, however, is to forget what is behind me and do my best to reach what is ahead" (Phil. 3:13, GNT).

When you pick up your mat, you begin a new chapter of your life, a new season of salvation, and a new journey of jubilation. Standing on your feet and walking by faith, picking up your mat and casting it aside, you signal to the world and everyone around you that you follow Jesus. You no longer cling to the past, but you engage the present in the presence of God, trusting Him for the fulfillment of your future.

When you pick up your mat and begin walking in the power of the Spirit, you telegraph to every devil, demon, legion, principality, and power of darkness that they no longer have any claim on you. You have been set free by the power of Jesus Christ! You do not live within their prisons of paralysis.

> You do not live in depression anymore.
> You do not live in failure anymore.
> You do not live in bitterness anymore.
> You do not live in anxiety anymore.
> You do not live in strife anymore.
> You do not live in chaos anymore.

How can you be sure you do not live there anymore? How can you refuse to turn and look behind you the way Lot's wife did and instead embrace your new identity, as did Gideon, Paul, Ruth, and so many others? How can you know the time has come to pick up your mat and surrender it at the foot of the cross? How can you live in the certainty that you will never go back to living a life of paralysis where you once were?

> The blood of Jesus says you do not live there anymore!
> The Spirit of God says you do not live there anymore!
> The Word of God says you do not live there anymore!
> You are not who you used to be!
> You were paralyzed, but now you can walk!
> You were lost, but now you are found!
> You were bound, but now you are free!

WALK THROUGH THAT DOOR

Some people have been believers so long that they act as if they never had a mat. They may have forgotten what it felt like to have a mat, or they may refuse to recognize their prior paralysis. They try to behave as if they have never been through anything messy, dirty, broken, or battered, which basically means they try to act as if they have never experienced real life!

Others attempt to follow Jesus but still lug their mats behind them like an old mattress. They know the Holy Spirit dwells within them and that Jesus has healed their paralysis, yet they continue to cling to remnants of their past, allowing old baggage to slow down their progress. Their mat might be an ongoing struggle to forgive someone who has offended or betrayed them. It might be feelings of shame or guilt over someone they themselves have hurt or betrayed.

Regardless of whether you struggle with the temptation to pretend you never had a mat or you still drag it behind you, you must acknowledge it, pick it up, and put it aside. The Bible reminds us, "Therefore, since we are surrounded by such a great cloud of witnesses, let us throw off everything that hinders and the sin that so easily entangles. And let us run with perseverance the race marked out for us" (Heb. 12:1). Allow God to transform your crutch into a cross.

In light of the abundance of blessings, in the face of such enormous healing, in consideration of all Christ has done for you, praise becomes the only fitting response. You must celebrate your new status with praise and thanksgiving, with joyful noise and worship music fit for the King! You see, praise expresses thanksgiving. I am convinced the size of your praise directly correlates to the magnitude of the hell you went through to get here now. The heights of your praise directly relate to the depths of the pit from which God took you. The sweetness of your praise directly corresponds to the bitterness of the storm He rescued you from.

You proportion the size of your praise according to your past paralysis!

Pick up your mat and walk as Jesus commands you. Obey your Master and honor your Savior through your loving response to His sacrifice on your behalf. Walk by faith and not by sight (2 Cor. 5:7). Walk in the Spirit and not in the flesh (Gal. 5:16).

> I am convinced the size of your praise directly correlates to the magnitude of the hell you went through to get here.

Do not waste any time. Walk by faith now.

I recently remembered this imperative to walk when I went shopping with Eva. As we approached the big box store, I watched a lady standing in front of the automatic doors with a confused look on her face. She did not know what to do.

Maybe you have had a similar experience. You head into a store when you suddenly stop and try to figure out how you get in. Then before you can think about it, the doors open by themselves. Maybe they startle you because you are thinking you have to open those doors yourself. Or perhaps you stand there out of range, waiting too far away to trigger them to open. Regardless, you simply have to walk through them. They wait to fling themselves wide, inviting you to step in.

My friend, right now you must walk through the doorway God has opened for you. You may have been straining and stretching to open the doors of your future for yourself. Or maybe you find yourself lingering, still processing the paralysis from which you have been delivered. My friend, you have been waiting for the doors to your future to open when God has been waiting for you to arrive! He has been waiting all along for you to get it, pick up your mat, let go of who you used to be, and embrace who He made you to be!

> Your season to walk has arrived!
> You no longer have to lie on the ground.
> You no longer have to crawl.
> You no longer have to writhe in the pain of the past.
> Put one foot in front of the other and walk!

You stand before the door of possibility, the door of the abundant life Jesus told us He came to bring. You stand before the door you had to fight to find. You stand before the door you had to overcome paralysis to reach, the door for which you had to defeat the powers of hell tugging at your legs and trying to bring you down.

But nothing can separate you from the love of Jesus Christ! Nothing!

> For I am convinced that neither death nor life, neither
> angels nor demons, neither the present nor the future,
> nor any powers, neither height nor depth, nor anything

else in all creation, will be able to separate us from the
love of God that is in Christ Jesus our Lord.

—ROMANS 8:38–39

Stand up.
Pick up your mat.
And start walking.
You.
Are.
Next!

Chapter Nine

YOU ARE NEXT...

TO RESPOND TO YOUR CRITICS

Don't let compliments get to your head
and don't let criticism get to your heart.
—LYSA TERKEURST

FTER YOU PICK up your mat and begin to walk, some people will cheer. Others will shrug as if they do not care. And some will actually get angry.

As my ministry began to grow along with the influence of the NHCLC, I soon discovered the impact poison can have on a healthy soul. This happened a number of years ago when social media was new, and being a tech nerd like I am, I embraced it immediately as an early adapter. The possibility of connecting with so many people—both Christians and nonbelievers, and not just in our country but around the world—genuinely excited me. So I helped create a website for our church, for NHCLC, and for myself. I joined Facebook and, appreciating the power a concisely worded thought can have, Twitter as well.

It took me less than a month to discover that despite my own enthusiasm I had inadvertently painted a virtual bull's-eye on my back. While hundreds and soon thousands of people let me know the messages and information provided online blessed them, another couple dozen seemed unimpressed or even livid. Based on their scathing comments, you would think I had posted the most vile, heretical expressions possible.

Some did not like my theology and the way I emphasized the role of the Holy Spirit in our personal relationship with God. Others questioned my sincerity and accused me of being out for their money. One even criticized my suit in the photo on my biography page! At first I tried to thoughtfully and prayerfully respond to their comments in a firm but loving way, indicating their mistakes and redirecting them to Scripture. This outraged half of them who couldn't believe I had dared to confront them. They countered with a mean-spirited negativity that shocked me.

But I quickly realized the problem in their responses. Not one of them seemed to have a legitimate basis for their critical response. They just liked finding someone to hate. They enjoyed expressing themselves to feel justified in their own beliefs. Like many critics do, they felt good about making others feel bad.

PRISM OF GOD'S POWER

Those social media posts were not the first time I drew criticism for my Christian faith, nor will they be the last. Jesus told us that as His followers we would attract criticism from other people—in fact, not just criticism but hatred. Christ said, "If the world hates you, keep in mind that it hated me first. If you belonged to the world, it would love you as its own. As it is, you do not belong to the world, but I have chosen you out of the world. That is why the world hates you" (John 15:18–19).

While He spoke these words to His disciples, Jesus could just as easily have said them to the man who was healed there beside the pool at Bethesda. Because after the man began to walk, the very fact of his miracle made others uncomfortable.

> At once the man was cured; he picked up his mat and walked.
>
> The day on which this took place was a Sabbath, and so the Jewish leaders said to the man who had been healed, "It is the Sabbath; the law forbids you to carry your mat."
>
> But he replied, "The man who made me well said to me, 'Pick up your mat and walk.'"

So they asked him, "Who is this fellow who told you to pick it up and walk?"

The man who was healed had no idea who it was, for Jesus had slipped away into the crowd that was there.

Later Jesus found him at the temple and said to him, "See, you are well again. Stop sinning or something worse may happen to you." The man went away and told the Jewish leaders that it was Jesus who had made him well.

—JOHN 5:9–15

Please keep in mind our setting. The pool at Bethesda, located near the Sheep Gate (v. 2), provided a place for cleansing prior to entering the temple there in Jerusalem. Verse 1 tells us that Jesus had traveled to the city for one of the Jewish festivals.

The Bible does not tell us which specific feast or festival, but we can assume it would most likely be one of three: the Festival of Unleavened Bread (Passover), held early in the spring; the Festival of Weeks (Pentecost), celebrated in late spring; or the Festival of Tabernacles, an early fall festival. Jews were obligated to visit the temple in Jerusalem for these three feasts according to God's instruction in Deuteronomy 16:16–17, so Jesus had traveled there accordingly.

I suspect that knowing the particular festival does not matter as much as simply setting the scene at festival time. Crowds of people would have been visiting the temple, with many from out of town. Perhaps there would have been even more pilgrims visiting the pool at Bethesda in hopes of securing a miracle for themselves after the angel stirred the waters. This might explain why the man did not seem alarmed by the presence of

Jesus. He likely saw Him as a visiting tourist performing His religious duty like thousands of others.

For Jewish religious leaders the busy festival time required their presence in full force. They not only needed to officiate and oversee the festival, but they also likely wanted to make the contrast between their righteousness and the uncleanness of the typical temple goer quite clear.

I am not merely speculating; I frequently see this motivation in the Jewish religious hierarchy's encounters with Jesus. The Pharisees, Sadducees, and other established religious leaders in Jesus' day prided themselves on their superiority. They were set apart from the average person because God had called and chosen them to serve Him in His temple.

Their status became a problem, however, when they stopped shining God's righteousness through their words and actions and instead turned the attention back on themselves. Instead of serving as a prism of God's power, they became paralyzed by looking at themselves in the mirror of merit.

FRICTION OF FAITH

When faced with such self-serving displays as the ones paraded by the Jewish religious leaders of His day, Christ quickly pointed out the problem. Nowhere, perhaps, do we find a sharper contrast than we see in this description.

> Then Jesus told this story to some who had great confidence in their own righteousness and scorned everyone else: "Two men went to the Temple to pray. One was a Pharisee, and the other was a despised tax collector. The Pharisee stood by himself and prayed this prayer:

'I thank you, God, that I am not like other people—cheaters, sinners, adulterers. I am certainly not like that tax collector! I fast twice a week, and I give you a tenth of my income.'

"But the tax collector stood at a distance and dared not even lift his eyes to heaven as he prayed. Instead, he beat his chest in sorrow, saying, 'O God, be merciful to me, for I am a sinner.' I tell you, this sinner, not the Pharisee, returned home justified before God. For those who exalt themselves will be humbled, and those who humble themselves will be exalted."

—LUKE 18:9–14, NLT

Can you imagine the audacity of your pastor pointing out his or her superiority in comparison to a member of the congregation? Because Jesus basically depicted that kind of scene in His description here—and what a difference in the two prayers the men prayed! The Pharisee stood up front and prayed loud enough for everyone to hear him, basically saying, "Thank You, Lord, that I am not like those nasty sinners I see everywhere—especially that tax collector over there! I obey You and do everything just right, as evidenced by how often I fast and how much money I give." The tax collector, on the other hand, kept his distance from others, stared down in humility, and beat his chest in sorrow as he whispered, "Dear God, please have mercy on me because I am a sinner!"

Now I would like to say that this kind of thing no longer happens in the modern, technologically advanced, culturally progressive world we live in today. But human nature never changes, and I have to say that some of the harshest, most abrasive, and most self-serving criticism I have ever received comes from people in positions of power and leadership. It seems they feel they can only maintain their status by putting others down.

But Jesus turned the tables on them here, just as He did throughout His entire ministry. At the conclusion of this story Christ said that the sinner, not the Pharisee, was right with God. And just to be sure everyone got the point, the Lord went on to put an exclamation point on His message by saying, "Those who exalt themselves will be humbled, and those who humble themselves will be exalted" (Luke 18:14, NLT).

My friend, you may feel as if you entered the race late because of your paralysis. You may believe that your faith will never be as strong as that of other Christians you know or that you can never study the Bible and understand it as well as pastors and leaders at your church. After all, you have had to deal with this debilitating paralysis most of your life. You have a lot of baggage. You come from the other side of the tracks. You have a dysfunctional family. You did not go to church growing up.

Eventually others will remind you of these points. They will try to disqualify your faith. "You have not studied theology the way I have," they might say. Or, "I have been a believer my whole life while you have only been a Christian a few months." Their words make you feel inferior, implying that somehow your relationship with God can never be as special, intimate, and strong as theirs.

But that is simply not true!

Like the perfect parent He is, God loves all His children uniquely and unconditionally. He does not play favorites. Or rather, according to Scripture and going back to what Jesus said, God favors the sinners who humbly and sorrowfully repent of their sins, ask for God's mercy, and receive His grace. The Bible makes it clear that all of us have sinned— every single human being that has ever drawn a breath!— and we fall short of the glory of God (Rom. 3:23). Not one of us will ever attain worthiness on our own merits! Our best efforts look like filthy rags compared to the righteousness of our most holy God (Isa. 64:6).

So it does not matter whether you have known Jesus for thirty years or thirty days—God loves you just the same. Whether you come from a trailer park or a gated community, God loves you just the same. Whether your parents were pastors or drug dealers, God loves you just the same. Whether you never finished high school or you have a PhD as the principal at a high school, God loves you just the same.

Each of us has sinned.

Each of us finds ourselves paralyzed.

Each of us needs a healing encounter with Jesus Christ!

And once we have felt new life course through our bodies, once we have picked up our mats, once we have started to put one foot in front of another on our new journey of faith, we will encounter resistance. No matter who you are, others will hate you for loving Jesus more than you love their approval.

So please do not be shocked, surprised, alarmed, or disappointed when your neighbor rebukes you, your coworker ignores you, or your friends condemn you. In fact, the Bible tells us to rejoice in such moments because they prove the real-life application of our faith. "That is why, for Christ's sake, I delight in weaknesses, in insults, in hardships, in persecutions, in difficulties. For when I am weak, then I am strong" (2 Cor. 12:10).

> **No matter who you are, others will hate you for loving Jesus more than you love their approval.**

Fact: critics will criticize you. Or as my kids like to say, "Haters gonna hate!" Their resistance has no power to invalidate your miracle—just the opposite! Their criticism creates friction that simply reveals your faith and the sparks of God's glory in your life.

ONCE BITTEN, TWICE SHY

Most critics often strike like a snake—with forked tongues full of venom. Just as serpents sinks their fangs into our ankles, critics aim low as well. They often like to catch us by surprise if possible, forcing us to react instead of respond. It reminds me of the old saying, "Once bitten, twice shy," which warns that we should know what to expect after we have been bitten at least once.

But not all critics venomously seek to destroy us—critical discourse can be a vital part of a thoughtful exchange of ideas. It all depends on the motivation behind the criticism, the manner in which they criticize, and the intended outcome. Based on my experience, I have identified at least three general categories for the kinds of critics we usually encounter.

Constructive critics

This first—and by far the most important—group of critics intend to challenge you, help you, and encourage you by telling you what needs to be said. Their words may be just as hard to hear as the harsh comments made by critics from the other groups, but constructive critics only want to make you stronger. Scripture consistently reminds us, "As iron sharpens iron, so one person sharpens another" (Prov. 27:17). And, "Wounds from a sincere friend are better than many kisses from an enemy" (Prov. 27:6, NLT).

Notice it goes back to the critic's motive in issuing the criticism. A sincere friend will not put you down just to make himself look good. He will not bully you for no reason or try to make you look foolish. Instead he might struggle to tell you the truth because he knows it will sting you, but being a true friend, he feels compelled to tell you the truth.

No matter how uncomfortable a friend might be in sharing his remarks, he knows that leaving things unsaid—or worse, telling you what you want to hear—is not really loving you well. Think about the friend who points out a piece of spinach stuck in your teeth! She probably feels embarrassed and awkward and does not like having to tell you. But the alternative, letting you leave the restaurant and go through the rest of your day with a green smile, seems far worse!

When I think of constructive critics, the prophet Nathan comes to mind and the way he handled the most difficult task of rebuking King David for his affair with Bathsheba and his responsibility in the death of her husband, Uriah. The Lord prompted Nathan to confront David, and the old prophet displayed sheer brilliance in the way he went about it. Knowing David would definitely not want to hear what Nathan had to say, the prophet instead chose to tell the king a story (2 Sam. 12).

Nathan's story revealed the crime that a rich man, who had many sheep and cattle in his pastures, committed against a poor man, who had only one ewe that had been treated more like a family pet than a main course (vv. 2–3). When a visitor came along, the rich man wanted to show hospitality by cooking a meal for his guest—only the wealthy host stole the poor man's only ewe and served it rather than choosing one of the many from his own flocks.

Understandably such flagrant injustice outraged David, and he demanded to know the identity of this reckless rich man so that he, as king, could punish the man's crime. And then Nathan tightened the noose around David's own neck! Obviously Nathan's story served as a metaphor for exactly what David had done. Hearing the situation from another, more objective vantage point, David could not deny his sin and asked for God's forgiveness.

I pray the constructive critics in your life never need to deliver such a story to you. But I do encourage you to keep your ears and heart open when—please pay attention to this—someone you know and trust shares criticism with the intention of building you up. This crucial kind of criticism does exactly that: it constructs and builds you up even if it feels as if your pride is being chipped away in the moment.

Welcome the criticism of true friends, and develop a strategy for dealing with all other critics. The next two categories of critics do the opposite of building you up. They intend to hasten your destruction, break you down, and destroy you.

Camouflaged critics

This second group of critics may be the most dangerous. Why? Because you might not readily identify them as your critics. These so-called friends intend their flattery, encouragement, and instruction to harm you without your knowledge. Camouflaged critics, like elite military operatives undercover in the jungle, tend to remain hidden as long as possible. They have their own an agenda and have simply caught you in the web they weave.

The person who betrayed Jesus exemplifies this more powerfully than anyone else. We think of Judas as the ultimate traitor—after all, we use his name as a synonym for *betrayer*. We can hardly imagine him as one of Jesus' closest friends, one of the twelve disciples handpicked by Christ to share His three years of public ministry on earth. The fact that Christ, as God and man, already knew in His sovereignty all that would happen only compounds the relationship between Jesus and Judas Iscariot.

And yet I believe Judas was more than an actor following a script. God in His vast and unlimited power certainly could have fulfilled the ancient prophecy regarding the Messiah's betrayal another way had Judas chosen differently. But as we know, Judas opened himself to the evil one, who entered him and fueled his scheme to hand Jesus over to the chief priests and officers of the temple guard (Luke 22:3–5). The Bible does not tell us any other motivation on Judas' part leading to this betrayal, but being human, we can imagine what it might have been.

Perhaps Judas felt jealous of Jesus' power, popularity, and passion for God. Judas might have been attracted to the limelight and ultimately wanted all the attention for himself. Maybe he never fully trusted Jesus and liked the idea of seeing the Master put to the ultimate test. Judas might have even thought of himself as a hero, saving the Jewish people from being conned by this carpenter claiming to be God's Son.

Another motive propelling Judas to give Satan a foothold into his heart might have been greed. Another reference in Scripture makes mention about Judas being the disciple in charge of the money (John 13:29). And of course money seemed to play a role because when the enemies of Jesus offered to pay Judas to tip them off, he gladly accepted. Luke's Gospel tells us, "And Judas went to the chief priests and the officers of the temple guard and discussed with them how he might betray Jesus. They were delighted and agreed to give him money. He consented, and watched for an opportunity to hand Jesus over to them when no crowd was present" (Luke 22:4–6).

The opportunity presented itself, of course, after the disciples had eaten the Passover meal with Jesus. At this gathering, known as the last supper, Jesus broke the bread and poured the wine, symbolizing His body and blood, and offered it to His disciples as a way to remember His sacrifice for them and their commitment to God. At the meal Christ told His followers that one of the twelve would imminently betray Him.

Even when Judas' Master clearly knew of his scheme, it did not deter his plans. Later that night, Jesus took some of the disciples to pray with Him in the Garden of Gethsemane, the perfect place to capture Jesus. Families likely gathered for their Passover meals, so very few people would be out and about so late at night. There would be no witnesses who might protest or give testimony about the trumped-up charges on which the religious leaders arrested Him.

Judas wasted no time in making the greatest mistake of his life. Luke's Gospel goes on to say, "While he was still speaking a crowd came up, and the man who was called Judas, one of the Twelve, was leading them. He approached Jesus to kiss him, but Jesus asked him, 'Judas, are you betraying the Son of Man with a kiss?'" (vv. 47–48).

Jesus' question here strikes me as very similar to the question the Lord asked the man at Bethesda—"Do you want to get well?" (John 5:6). Basically Jesus asked another question with such an obvious answer as to be rhetorical in nature. Knowing full well that Judas planned to betray Him with a kiss, Jesus still directed this question directly to His disciple. While we cannot know for sure, I suspect the reason had to do with responsibility. I see it as a case in which Jesus basically said, "Judas, you realize what you are doing here, right? Undoubtedly, if you greet Me with a kiss, these Roman guards will arrest Me."

On a much smaller scale the situation reminds me of when our kids were young. Eva or I would catch one of them just about to do something they had been forbidden to do—jump off the back of the couch, say, or sample the cake on the kitchen counter before dinner. We would say, "You realize that if you go ahead and do what you are about to do that there will be consequences, right?"

In these moments, Jesus reminds us that all camouflaged critics will eventually be revealed. As you may know, Judas' story did not have a happy ending as he faced the unbearable consequences of his actions.

When Judas, who had betrayed him, saw that Jesus was condemned, he was seized with remorse and returned the thirty pieces of silver to the chief priests and the elders. "I have sinned," he said, "for I have betrayed innocent blood."

"What is that to us?" they replied. "That is your responsibility."

So Judas threw the money into the temple and left. Then he went away and hanged himself.

—MATTHEW 27:3–5

Cancerous critics

This final group of critics may be camouflaged at times, just as cancer cells in the body may go undetected for a while, but usually these critics do not mind attacking you directly. They intend to sow seeds of discord and want to cause problems in their assault on you and your purpose. This group—again, like the deadly disease that continues to claim millions of lives around the world—never really goes away. Once they get started, they will often pop up to thwart you again and again.

We see this type of critic in the chief priests and Pharisees who plagued Jesus throughout His entire ministry. In addition to the scene we looked at previously, Christ had even stronger words for this group: "Woe to you, teachers of the law and Pharisees, you hypocrites! You shut the door of the kingdom of heaven in people's faces. You yourselves do not enter, nor will you let those enter who are trying to" (Matt. 23:13).

Jesus went on to call them whitewashed tombs that appear as smooth as stone on the outside but are full of decaying bones on the inside. He also called them dirty cups that appear clean

outwardly but are disgusting inside. He said to consider can-
cerous critics like these as nothing more than snakes, broods
of vipers that writhe and strike at the heels of others. Christ
condemned them in no uncertain terms and left no doubt
about their destination in the afterlife (vv. 14–39).

To deal with this group of critics, distance yourself as
quickly as possible. I do not mean that you should ignore them,
because you ignore them at your own peril. Instead you must
confront them at times, just as Jesus did, and speak truth to
them in the loving authority of the Holy Spirit. But you must
never let them distract you or divert your attention from your
relationship with God and His purpose for you.

The devil loves to use these deadly critics to consume your
energy and occupy your time. If you feel upset and afraid
because you have others cutting into you with their words
and deeds, then you will end up becoming defensive. And
when you feel defensive, you will put up walls to attempt to
keep other people out. You will become quick to judge and
assess others, sometimes accurately but other times incor-
rectly. You will close yourself off and live in fear rather than
walk by faith.

But you actually do not live at all—you end up right back
in paralysis. It might be a different kind of wound, but many
critics nonetheless want to stop you in your tracks, just as they
attempted with the paralyzed man in John chapter 5. "Who
do you think you are?" they asked him. "Don't you know it is
the Sabbath and you are not allowed to carry a mat on the
Sabbath?"

I love our healed hero's reply: "Uh, the guy over there said
to pick up my mat and walk, so that is what I am doing!" The

Jewish religious leaders then smelled trouble and asked, "What guy?" The newly healed man did not even know his healer's name—not until later when Jesus sought him out in the temple and told him, "See, you are well again. Stop sinning or something worse may happen to you" (John 5:14).

We do not know if Jesus addressed something specific at that moment or if He spoke broadly about how the man should live the rest of his life. Either way we get the same message: do not return to a life paralyzed by sin once Jesus has told you to pick up your mat and walk.

Once God has healed you, do not waste your time hobbling!

HEALED, HOLY, HAPPY

After learning who had healed him, the previously paralyzed man knew what he had to do: "The man went away and told the Jewish leaders that it was Jesus who had made him well" (John 5:15). I do not believe the man went to report Jesus' name to Christ's enemies because he feared them. I believe the man wanted to give credit where credit was due! He wanted everyone to know the name of Jesus Christ, the Son of God who had instantly healed him.

We should speak the truth to our critics with the same boldness. Just as the man's mat, which he obviously no longer needed, caught the attention of the religious legalists out to patrol for any violators, what we carry as we walk by faith should cause others to take notice. What you carry must provoke those you encounter to say, "Who gives you authority?"

What you carry must be provocative!

What you carry should disturb the status quo!

What you carry needs to call attention to the One who healed you!

Stop and think for a moment: Who has the right to question you about your faith, your family, your future? Who can stop you from carrying your old mat, whatever you used to depend upon for comfort that you no longer need? Who has the right to tell you what you can and cannot do in the power of Jesus?

This man declared, "He who healed me gave me the right!"

In other words, when Satan, his minions, other people used by him, those ignorant of your situation, or deadly critics attempt to dictate what you carry, you need to let them know who healed you. When they try to interfere with your divine destiny, get up and tell them what the man who had been paralyzed for thirty-eight years prior to his healing encounter with Jesus said: If you did not heal me...if you did not save me...if you did not deliver me...if you did not set me free...then you do not have the right to tell me what I can or cannot carry! The One who healed me gave me the right and told me to carry this!

You only need to carry what Jesus tells you to carry. No one else gets to tell you what you can or cannot carry. No one else saved you, healed you, loved you, and empowered you.

Therefore, no one else can prevent you from enjoying the abundant life Jesus came to bring. God calls you to walk by faith, not wallow in the paralysis of the past. You have the right to be full of joy because Jesus told you to walk. You have the right to live a holy, healed, healthy, happy, humble life because Jesus told you to stand up, pick up your mat, and walk!

Any time a critic makes you doubt your identity, purpose, or destination, remember the Lord's promise: "But you belong to God, my dear children. You have already won a victory over those people, because the Spirit who lives in you is greater than the spirit who lives in the world" (1 John 4:4, NLT).

God has placed far greater things *in* you than what the devil has placed in front of you. If their praise did not make you, then their criticism cannot break you. You have everything you need inside you—right here, right now. Never allow anyone to tell you otherwise! If they try to stop you, tell them you only do what Jesus told you to do. You only take orders from Him!

My friend, when you walk by faith, your critics have no authority to stop you.

> **God has placed far greater things *in* you than what the devil has placed in front of you.**

They momentarily slow you down but only long enough for you to speak the name of Jesus! You have been healed and no longer wait for others to do what only God Himself has done. Shake off the critics, and stand up and walk!

You are next!

Chapter Ten

YOU ARE NEXT...

EVEN ON THE SABBATH!

It's never too late for a new
beginning in your life.
—JOYCE MEYER

W HEN I GREW up in Pennsylvania, most stores did not open on Sundays. People went to church or slept in or went to Pittsburgh to watch the Steelers play. We knew an older man in our neighborhood who got upset if anyone mowed their lawn on Sunday, even a push mower rather than a loud, gas-powered one. In our own family, Sundays were for faith, food, and *familia*. We would go to church and then enjoy an incredible spread of delicious food my mother, grandmother, and aunts cooked for us.

We would savor an amazing feast featuring many Puerto Rican dishes that remain my favorites today. We would have smoked pork loin or roasted chicken served with *arroz con gandules* (a traditional dish of rice with pigeon peas), *rellenos de papa* (fried, stuffed, spicy mashed potatoes), *frijoles con tocino* (slow-simmered beans with bacon), and *tostones* (sliced plantains seasoned and deep fried in oil). With such a mouthwatering meal to anticipate each week, you can understand why I remember Sunday as my favorite day!

For many of us Sunday has now become just another day of the week. Maybe we do not have to work in the office or punch our time card, but so much still needs to be done in preparation for the rest of the week. Most stores have regular hours of operation, that is, if you do not want to stay home and shop online. Even if you go to church on Sundays, and I hope you do or that you go sometime during your week, then it can still feel like a busy day.

As a pastor I view Sundays as a special kind of workday. I have always believed that during our congregation's time to gather for worship and to experience God's message from the

Word, the rest of the week's work comes together. Like a marathon, when you run on race day, you celebrate all the training and hard work you have put into preparing for that day. You do not wake up on race day and decide to run a marathon.

And when our kids were young, I believe my wife and I sometimes felt as if we were running a marathon. Eva would make sure everyone ate breakfast while I helped get them all bathed and dressed, even as I made last-minute changes to my sermon. Back in those days, getting us all to church on time felt like herding cats in a hailstorm! We can look back nostalgically on those times now that our kids have grown, but at the time, it sometimes stretched our patience beyond our limits. Yes, Sundays will always hold a special place in my life.

As special as Sundays are, however, they can sometimes get in the way of knowing God. Just ask the paralyzed man!

SABBATH SATISFACTION

In the previous chapter we explored how we will always attract critics once we begin walking in faith and obeying the voice of Jesus, just as the paralyzed man did after being healed of his paralysis. You will recall the setting: festival time in Jerusalem with thousands of people crowding their way in and around the temple. Consequently the temple priests and religious leaders seemed to have been on the lookout for anything or anyone not adhering to the strict Jewish Law. So when they saw the paralyzed man skipping along and carrying his mat on a Sabbath, a direct violation of their interpretation of the Mosaic Law, they got in his path and quizzed him.

The man did not argue or disagree with them. At first not knowing the identity of the stranger who had healed him and instructed him to carry his mat and walk, the man simply explained as much to the temple patrol posse wanting to give him a citation. A short while later Jesus sought out the man there in the temple and warned him to recognize the fullness of his healing by no longer living a life crippled by sin. The man must have taken the Savior's words to heart because he immediately found his inquisitors and made sure they knew who had healed him: Jesus Christ!

He started a chain reaction. The Jewish temple priests and religious leaders must have thought they finally had Jesus cornered. I am sure you can imagine them saying, "Aha! We have Him now! That carpenter from Nazareth again, the One claiming to be the Messiah. Well, if He were really God's Son, He would know better than to heal someone on a Sabbath and tell that person to carry his mat! Yes, we will just see what this Jesus has to say about that!" Basically, as we see here, they looked for any excuse to trip Him up.

> So, because Jesus was doing these things on the Sabbath, the Jewish leaders began to persecute him. In his defense Jesus said to them, "My Father is always at his work to this very day, and I too am working." For this reason they tried all the more to kill him; not only was he breaking the Sabbath, but he was even calling God his own Father, making himself equal with God.
>
> —JOHN 5:16–18

Notice what Jesus says in response to their persecution about the Sabbath: "My father is *always* at his work *to this very day*, and I too am working" (v. 17, emphasis added). Two things stand out here. First, Jesus beat them at their own legalistic game. God exists outside of time as we know it and is always at work. These traits inherently make up in His identity. In other words, God does not stop working on the Sabbath even though He did set a precedent for us humans by resting on the seventh day after creation (Gen. 2:2)—more on that momentarily. So if God never rests and always works, which the religious leaders could not refute, then He obviously worked on that very day.

Second, Jesus spoke the truth of His identity without making that the center of His defense. He told the religious guys that just as God worked all the time, so did He. And by the way, God just happened to be His father. Without necessarily trying to provoke them, Christ surely knew the effect His explanation would have on these self-righteous legalists. They not only hated Him more—they wanted to kill Him even more than before. How dare He claim to be the Son of God! Who would dare make such outrageous claims as to set Himself up as equal to our heavenly Father?

Once again in His ministry Jesus made it clear that He came to upset the usual order of expectations and traditional adherence to past ordinances. No one born on earth had more claim to being a king, and yet Jesus' birth had been humbler than anything even some of the poorest people would have experienced then. Mary gave birth to Christ our King on the edge of the backwater town of Bethlehem in a cowshed, of all places!

The Bible says nothing of a palace, earthly royal fanfare, or a lavish welcoming party. Instead it speaks of a manger, the heavenly host, and shepherds. The event went against everything a good Jewish person would have expected concerning the arrival of the Messiah. With this arrival into our world Jesus began revealing a pattern that characterized His entire life on earth.

FAITH IN FLIGHT

Christ never tried to hide His defiance of conventional expectations either. He not only boldly proclaimed to be the Son of God, but He also made it clear that His presence would disrupt the religious sensibilities of that time. Jesus stated it clearly enough.

> Do not suppose that I have come to bring peace to the earth. I did not come to bring peace, but a sword. For I have come to turn "a man against his father, a daughter against her mother, a daughter-in-law against her mother-in-law—a man's enemies will be the members of his own household."
>
> Anyone who loves their father or mother more than me is not worthy of me; anyone who loves their son or daughter more than me is not worthy of me. Whoever does not take up their cross and follow me is not worthy of me. Whoever finds their life will lose it, and whoever loses their life for my sake will find it.
>
> —MATTHEW 10:34–39

Some people hearing Jesus might have assumed He meant He came to bring a military coup against the Roman Empire in order to free Israel and restore it to its former glory. Others would have been troubled by Christ's words here because even if He planned to conquer the Romans, they would have expected the Son of God to establish peace eventually. Instead Jesus went on and on about how much personal strife His presence on earth would cause!

In mentioning the impact His presence on earth would have on various family relationships, Jesus quoted the prophet Micah, who warned against trusting anyone completely, even close family members in one's own household (Mic. 7:5–6). In the verse after this reference, however, Micah concluded, "But as for me, I watch in hope for the LORD, I wait for God my Savior; my God will hear me" (v. 7).

The emphasis in both Jesus' declaration and the passage from Micah stresses the individual's relationship with God, the need for a Savior, and God's provision. Many in Jesus' audience would have recognized the quotation from Micah and would have seen the way Jesus fulfilled the prophet's centuries-old prayer.

The issue then became a matter of His listeners letting go of their expectations and embracing who Jesus was rather than who they wanted Him to be. This dilemma was at the crux of the conflict ignited by the religious leaders. They had convinced themselves they were so righteous and holy that they would be sure to recognize the Messiah when God sent Him. They could not see their own pride, arrogance, and self-righteousness, which blinded them from recognizing the deity of Jesus.

Many people still have this same struggle today. They cannot imagine God any other way than as they want Him to be. So they close themselves to anything dissimilar to what they already believe and want to see. God is, if anything, mysterious. His ways are not our ways. His power, wisdom, and authority transcend anything we can grasp. We are His creation, and He is our Creator.

If we want to truly experience the abundance of life Jesus brings, we must be willing to let go of our own expectations. Even after we have encountered Christ and walked with Him for a long time, we must never assume God conforms to our way of seeing things or our timetable for answering prayers. Our spiritual growth depends on humility. Just as the man healed from his paralysis could not wait to go find the religious leaders and let them know who healed him, so we too must express the full identity of our Savior.

Human systems, temporal progression, and what we think of as scientific fact do not confine God. While an orthopedic specialist from the twenty-first century might be able to examine the paralyzed man before and after his healing to attempt a medical explanation of what took place, we should not need to understand how God's miracles happen in order to receive them in our lives.

> **If we want to truly experience the abundance of life Jesus brings, we must be willing to let go of our own expectations.**

I fly thousands of miles each year, choosing to board a giant metal bird hurtling through the sky at hundreds of miles per hour. While I have a basic understanding of how planes work and the engineering aerodynamics of flight, I do not know all the details of what makes a 747 function properly. I simply trust that the plane works adequately and the pilots have enough experience to transport the other passengers and me to our destination. I suspect when you fly, you likely exercise the same kind of trust.

If we can travel nearly forty thousand feet above the earth's surface based on trusting other humans, should we not be willing to put our faith in God without understanding how—or even why—He does everything He does?

LIBERTY FROM LEGALISM

I understand the importance of obeying God's commands fully and completely. One of the Ten Commandments focuses on this very issue of the Sabbath and our response to it. "Remember the Sabbath day by keeping it holy," Exodus 20:8 tells us, followed by more specific instructions on what it means to honor God on this special day. The Scripture also says, "But the seventh day is a sabbath to the LORD your God. On it you shall not do any work, neither you, nor your son or daughter, nor your male or female servant, nor your ox, your donkey or any of your animals, nor any foreigner residing in your towns, so that your male and female servants may rest, as you do" (Deut. 5:14).

Sabbath does not mean Saturday in Hebrew, as one might be tempted to guess. Instead it derives from the Hebrew *shabbath*, which simply means rest, thereby explaining the dramatic emphasis on rest in the verse above. In biblical times the Israelites set aside the seventh and final day of the week, which we call Saturday, as this day of rest. Consequently Jewish people had to prepare extra food and complete household chores before sundown on the sixth day, when their Sabbath began.

Knowing a little background on honoring the Sabbath helps us to understand why these religious leaders took the Mosaic Law so seriously and expected others to do so as well. I believe God wants us to obey His command even today and observe a day of rest during which we unplug and recharge by focusing only on Him. But as the Bible makes clear, the religious leaders were not motivated by a desire for respectful obedience. No, they had simply discovered a convenient trap to use in their attempts to paint Jesus into a corner. Not only that, adherence to the Sabbath became an issue in other instances as well, as Mark recorded in his Gospel.

> One Sabbath Jesus was going through the grainfields, and as his disciples walked along, they began to pick some heads of grain. The Pharisees said to him, "Look, why are they doing what is unlawful on the Sabbath?"
>
> He answered, "Have you never read what David did when he and his companions were hungry and in need? In the days of Abiathar the high priest, he entered the house of God and ate the consecrated bread, which is lawful only for priests to eat. And he also gave some to his companions."
>
> Then he said to them, "The Sabbath was made for man, not man for the Sabbath. So the Son of Man is Lord even of the Sabbath."
>
> —MARK 2:23–28

Once again Jesus beat these Pharisees and religious leaders at their own game. When they confronted Him about the unlawful grain picking His disciples did on the Sabbath, Jesus referenced another historical incident in which someone had ostensibly broken the law under circumstances virtually every rabbi considered justifiable (1 Sam. 21:1–6). David and his men not only violated the law but also did something more unbelievable: ate bread consecrated in the temple, which only priests could eat!

Jesus then summed up the entire issue for these religious leaders just to make it clear: "The Sabbath was made *for man*, not man for *the Sabbath*" (Mark 2:27, emphasis added). He stated the fundamental problem with legalism in a nutshell. Unswerving obedience and adherence to the Law had become more important than the reason for the Law's observance in the first place. Ironically the Pharisees violated the Sabbath by being more concerned with confronting and trapping Jesus than with what they should be doing if they truly wanted to honor the Sabbath: resting.

The last word on the matter belonged to Christ as well: "The Son of Man is Lord even of the Sabbath" (v. 28). In other words, God cannot be confined by the laws, expectations, and precedents that human beings hold—even if those observances intend to show Him our respect! The Jewish leaders foolishly placed their authority and righteousness above God's. They refused to see Jesus for who He was and to hear what He had to say to them. So they tried to restrict Him, but they could not.

When God wants to heal you, you are next—even on the Sabbath!

NEVER TOO LATE

Jesus dramatically proved His identity as the Messiah, the Son of God, sent to save His people from their sins. But He did not sacrifice Himself and atone for our sins in the way even His closest disciples expected. Whether they thought He would supernaturally install Himself as Israel's new king or simply establish a more grassroots kingdom based on His growing popularity and dramatic healings, the disciples must have been shocked when their friend, their Lord, their Master, told them what was about to happen.

Not only would He be falsely accused and arrested, but also He would be executed for no good reason. And then wide eyed and terrified, the apostles watched as the One who healed the paralyzed man and calmed the stormy sea died the most agonizing death possible while nailed to a rough crossbeam of wood like a common criminal. How could this have happened? I wonder if they secretly asked the same questions that the Roman guards used to taunt Jesus: "If You are really the King of the Jews, then why do You not come down off that cross and save Yourself?"

Instead the disciples saw Jesus' lifeless body taken down. They saw His body wrapped in a shroud for burial in a borrowed tomb. He was God in human form! But now, no longer alive, He looked like any other mortal who could not defeat the inevitable frailty of flesh and blood.

Or could He? Because as we know, Jesus defeated death once and for all! They crucified Him and He died on a Friday, which we know because the Jews eagerly made sure He and the two criminals beside Him were dead and disposed of prior to sundown, which signaled the beginning of the Sabbath. Then Jesus' cold and lifeless body lay still within a stone cave sealed by a giant boulder. In death, Jesus obeyed the Sabbath. His dead body did not move, and He rested.

But not for long. At some point after the Sabbath passed, around dawn of the third day, Christ's resurrected body exited the tomb for all eternity! Even this revelation went against what we might expect. Instead of making a huge, larger-than-life announcement of His resurrection to His disciples, instead of laughing in the face of the Jewish religious leaders and passive Roman officials who put Him to death, Jesus chose a most surprising audience for His first appearance.

> After the Sabbath, at dawn on the first day of the week, Mary Magdalene and the other Mary went to look at the tomb.
>
> There was a violent earthquake, for an angel of the Lord came down from heaven and, going to the tomb, rolled back the stone and sat on it. His appearance was like lightning, and his clothes were white as snow. The guards were so afraid of him that they shook and became like dead men.
>
> The angel said to the women, "Do not be afraid, for I know that you are looking for Jesus, who was crucified. He is not here; he has risen, just as he said. Come and see the place where he lay. Then go quickly and tell his disciples: 'He has risen from the dead and is going ahead of you into Galilee. There you will see him.' Now I have told you."
>
> So the women hurried away from the tomb, afraid yet filled with joy, and ran to tell his disciples. Suddenly Jesus met them. "Greetings," he said. They came to him,

clasped his feet and worshiped him. Then Jesus said to
them, "Do not be afraid. Go and tell my brothers to go to
Galilee; there they will see me."

—MATTHEW 28:1–10

Jesus chose two ordinary women, one of whom probably had
some baggage from her past before meeting her Savior. Keep in
mind that this culture did not have high regard for women. Yet
these women chose to go and attend to their beloved friend's
body, intending to anoint it with herbs and balms to impede
the stench of decay. Their task served as a grim, humbling
reminder of the frail mortality that resulted in the death of the
Master they had so believed in.

Imagine their surprise when they arrived, dejected and
downcast, perhaps even paralyzed by their own displacement
now that the center of their world was gone. Suddenly an earth-
quake occurred and an angel appeared! The guards, stationed
at the tomb to make sure no one attempted to steal Jesus' body
and perpetuate the rumor that He had arisen, passed out like
dead men. The women, scared and shaky, followed the angel's
instruction to go and tell the disciples.

Before the women got to the disciples, however, the Lord
Himself intercepted them! They immediately fell to the ground
and worshipped Him. In many ways we have come full circle in
this book, and we end where we began, on the ground looking
up at Jesus—only what a difference this time! The paralyzed
man did not even know who this stranger was; he simply knew
that when he did what this person told him to do, he was
healed! He could walk again. So he did as the man asked and
picked up his mat and began walking into the temple.

The two women here, Mary and Mary Magdalene, fell to the ground, not because of paralysis but because they too were healed in an instant. Their faith and hope were restored. Jesus was indeed who He claimed to be: the Christ, the Messiah, the Son of God now risen from the dead. Their trust in Him was not misplaced.

And neither has yours, my friend.

No matter what your position in life, no matter what you may have done, no matter what disease you may be battling or what addiction you may be fighting, simply look to the Lord. He is alive and filled with power! He wants to heal you and give you the gift of His Holy Spirit to dwell in you, to be your Comforter and Friend, your Advocate with the Father. If you take nothing else from our time together between these pages, I pray you will realize that it is never too late for your miracle!

> You may have been waiting seven hours, seventeen days, or seventy years.
> You may not be able to imagine how your circumstances could ever change.
> You may be so tired of hoping that you no longer try to believe your life will ever be any different.

My friend, I have only one thing to say to you: Do. Not. Give. Up. Do not give up! Your journey will go on, and your healing has already begun! You are next—even if you do not feel like it right now. God has never given up on you. Do not give up on God!

"BUT WAIT! THERE'S MORE!"

Why am I so sure that God has more in store for you? How do I know He wants to revive you, restore you, heal you, and reveal you? Because God enjoys doing the impossible! He loves doing what no man or woman could ever do; it forces people to recognize His power, His glory, and His goodness.

If the paralyzed man had known who Jesus was, if while lying there on the ground by the pool at Bethesda he had heard the rumors of this man from Nazareth who had been healing others, I wonder if the man would have dared to consider that Jesus might heal him. We have already seen how the paralyzed man, at best, only seemed to hope for what he could imagine—that someone would help him get in the pool faster than anyone else.

But apparently this had not happened in the years—if not decades—that he had been going there. He simply moved too slowly. His legs did not work. He really could not find a way. Still, some spark of hope must have resided in this man's soul or he would not have remained at the pool, daring to believe it could happen even though he could not imagine how.

The festival had brought many visitors to Jerusalem. And they continued to crowd around and jostle along the periphery of the temple as they waited to enter. But most still avoided doing anything they did not have to do in accordance with the Mosaic Law on the Sabbath. If this Jesus could heal him, the man would assume that Christ would not do it on the Sabbath in accordance with the Law.

But this miracle happened on the Sabbath!

Think about this word *but* for a moment. Remember the old *Schoolhouse Rock!* TV spots? If I am referencing something before your time, you can Google it! But one of these short little educational cartoons asked, "Conjunction Junction, what's your function?" It taught kids the grammatical function of conjunctions—linking up words and phrases and clauses—in a very entertaining way. The wonderful conjunction *but* sets up contrast. If you want to join two or more words, go with *and*. If you want to provide different options, then *or* works very well.

> **God will work His purposes in your life even when people say He is not supposed to do it.**

Using *but* signals that what follows after it counters what went before it. In this case, saying, "The paralyzed man's miracle occurred, *but* it happened on the Sabbath!" indicates that it happened then even though apparently it was not supposed to happen then!

What does this mean? It means God will work His purposes in your life even when people say He is not supposed to do it. It means in the midst of your paralysis God will perform the miracle everyone deems impossible.

God will do it when all of hell says He is not supposed to do it.

God will do it when your flesh says He is not supposed to do it.

God will do it when your circumstances say He is not
 supposed to do it.
God will do it when your past says He is not supposed to
 do it.
He will do it on the Sabbath.
He will do it in the midst of the storm.
He will do it in the fiery furnace.
Neither the Sabbath nor anything else can limit our God!

I have experienced God's power to transcend the Sabbath
and do what He wants when He wants so many times. One
of the most visible and dramatic instances happened when
the executive committee for President Trump's inauguration
asked me to participate in the event. I had not actively sup-
ported Trump's candidacy or any other party's candidates. As
I frequently say, I do not support the donkey or the elephant—I
support the Lamb! Nonetheless, many peers and even friends
of mine told me that in no way would I be asked to be involved
in such a dramatic event without already being an insider.

In fact, because I had been involved in President Obama's
White House Task Force on Fatherhood and Healthy Families,
I knew many people might think my political perspective
leaned in his party's direction. While I worked hard to make it
clear I was genuinely nonpartisan, because I had also met with
President George W. Bush during his time in office, I realized
the executive committee for President Trump's inauguration
might not see this and would instead go with more familiar
pastors and Christian leaders.

Then the call came asking if I would be willing to offer a
prayer from the podium during the actual inauguration

ceremony. It floored me! Even if I had been the new president's campaign manager, I would never have expected such an honor. Once again, I sensed God's favor upon me. I did nothing to deserve such a platform, yet I would be seen by millions of people around the world in the televised coverage of this event.

I had thought I missed my turn.

I had thought my past had paralyzed me.

I had thought I should not try to do what I could not do before.

But God asked me to obey and not worry about what anyone else said. He asked me to take His hand, rise to my feet, and walk by faith. He told me to pick up my mat, shake off old excuses, and let Him transform my mat into His miracle. And guess what?

You are next!

> We cannot call it a miracle if we can make it or predict it on our own.

What God does next in your life will anger hell, upset the legalists around you, send other believers into spontaneous praise, and give you a testimony that will change your life. You will be walking in the Spirit in the fullness of what Jesus has done in your life. You will be telling others as I am telling you: *it is your turn!* Even if it is not supposed to happen—perhaps *especially* if it is not supposed to happen! After all, we cannot call it a miracle if we can make it or predict it on our own.

The paralyzed man encountered Jesus, and his life changed forever. His miracle happened when it should not have happened. His miracle happened when the Pharisees said it should not happen. It happened when the culture did not believe it could happen.

And now it will happen for you! No excuses, no turning back. Leave paralysis in the past. Faith in Jesus Christ fuels your future. Do you want to get well, my friend? Then allow me to say it one last time:

YOU ARE NEXT!

NOTES

CHAPTER 2

1.   Frances J. Crosby, "Blessed Assurance," 1873, https://library
.timelesstruths.org/music/Blessed_Assurance/.

2.   Edward Everett Hale, quoted in Edwin Osgood Grover, ed.,
The Book of Good Cheer: A Little Bundle of Cheery Thoughts (Chicago:
P. F. Volland & Company, 1909), 28, https://books.google.com
/books?id=v8sVAAAAYAAJ&q.

CHAPTER 4

1.   Samuel Rodriguez, *Shake Free: How to Deal With the Storms,
Shipwrecks, and Snakes in Your Life* (New York: WaterBrook, 2018).

CHAPTER 7

1.   C. S. Lewis, *The Great Divorce* (New York, NY: HarperCollins,
2009), 112.

CHAPTER 8

1.   Kyle Chayka, "The Oppressive Gospel of 'Minimalism,'" *The
New York Times Magazine*, July 26, 2016, http://www.nytimes.com
/2016/07/31/magazine/the-oppressive-gospel-of-minimalism.html.

ABOUT THE AUTHOR

Rev. Dr. Samuel Rodriguez is the president of the National Hispanic Christian Leadership Conference (NHCLC), the world's largest Hispanic Christian organization with over forty thousand US churches and over 450,000 churches spread throughout the Spanish-speaking diaspora. Rodriguez was named among the "Top 100 Christian Leaders in America" by Newsmax in 2015 and nominated for *Time*'s "100 Most Influential People in the World" in 2013. Rodriguez is regularly seen on CNN, Fox News, Univision, and PBS, and he has been featured in *Time*, *Christianity Today*, the *New York Times*, and the *Wall Street Journal*.

Rodriguez was the first Latino to deliver the keynote address at the Martin Luther King Jr. Annual Commemorative Service at Ebenezer Baptist Church; was a recipient of the Martin Luther King Jr. Leadership Award presented by the Congress of Racial Equality; and was a recipient of the Defender of the Dream Award presented in 2016 by Alveda King and the King family. Rodriguez has advised Presidents Bush, Obama, and Trump, and he frequently consults with Congress, advancing immigration and criminal justice reform as well as various pro-life and religious freedom initiatives. On January 20, 2017, with millions of people watching around the world, Rev. Rodriguez became the first Latino Evangelical to participate in a presidential inauguration, reading a passage from Matthew 5.

Rodriguez is executive producer of two films (*Flamin' Hot* and *The Impossible*) in partnership with Franklin Entertainment and 20th Century Fox. He likewise serves as cofounder and lead pastor of TBN Salsa, an international Christian-based broadcast television network. He is the author of *Shake Free*, as well as *Be Light*, a *Los Angeles Times* number one best seller.

Rodriguez serves as Senior Pastor of New Season Christian Worship Center in Sacramento, California, where he resides with his wife, Eva, and their three children.

PastorSam.com
NewSeasonWorship.org
Twitter: Samuel Rodriguez @NHCLC
Facebook: RevSamuelRodriguez
Podcast on iTunes and Spotify: Pastor Samuel Rodriguez
YouTube: Pastor Samuel Rodriguez
Instagram: PastorSamuelRodriguez

National Hispanic Christian Leadership Conference
PO Box 293389
Sacramento, CA 95829
(916) 919-7476